Pocket Guide to Hiring Geeks

42 Tips and Real-World Stories

on How to Read Resumes Brilliantly,

Conduct Effective Technical Interviews,

and Hire Exactly the Right People.

by Bill Holtsnider and George Stragand

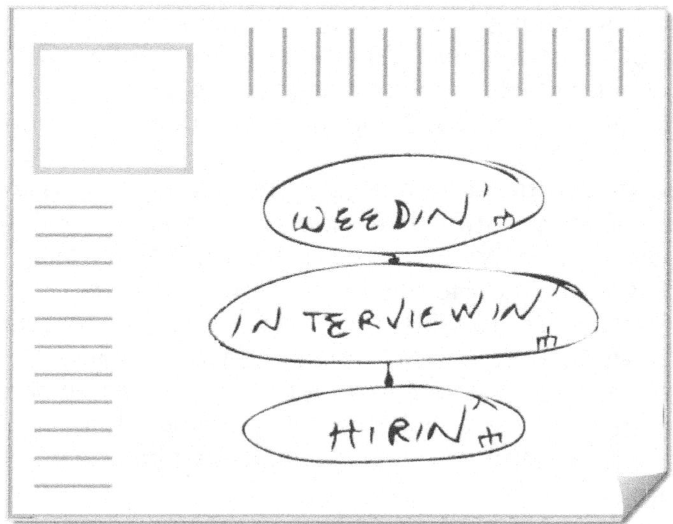

For further details, see PocketGuideToHiringGeeks.com.

Dedications

Bill H: For S: It is a great privilege to know you.

George S: 4 Elf BFF

Special thanks to Kim Lindeen and MNG, the CreateSpace editor for their great work on copy editing this book.

About the Authors

Bill Holtsnider (pg2hgbh@gmail.com) is an experienced writer, educator, and software professional with more than 28 years of experience working in the computer industry. His IT expertise includes working in such diverse areas as stock portfolio management, Web analytics and software development. He is the author of seven books and a wide range of technical and marketing documentation.

George Stragand (george@georgestragand.com) is a manager and software developer with over 20 years of producing and managing the delivery of commercial software on time. He has worked for companies ranging in size from start-ups to multinationals, creating software for both external and in-house use. He still hasn't found a problem that couldn't be solved by one more level of indirection or a suitable amount of explosives in the correct location, except maybe a whale.

Contents

Introduction to Hiring Geeks — 7

Why You Have to Do This — 11

Section A: Weedin'

Tip 1: Always be Looking for Superior Talent. Always. — 21

Tip 2: Talk to HR—or Not — 25

Tip 3: How to Get Help with Your Hiring — 29

Tip 4: Internal Hires — 33

Tip 5: How to Hire Someone Who Has More Technical Knowledge than You — 37

Tip 6: Consultant or Employee? — 43

Tip 7: Write Down a Job Description — 49

Tip 8: Using Social Networking — 55

Tip 9: Network Your A Off** — 61

Tip 10: The Good, Bad and Ugly about Using Recruiters — 65

Tip 11: How to Read a Resume — 71

Tip 12: Narrowing Down the List (Initial Step) — 77

Tip 13: Should You Hire an Overqualified Candidate? — 83

Section B: Interviewin'

Tip 14: Conduct the Best Type of Interview	89
Tip 15: Useful Interview Guidelines	95
Tip 16: Let Management Know What You Need	101
Tip 17: How to Greet Interviewees	105
Tip 18: Prepare a List of Questions in Advance	109
Tip 19: Basic Questions to Cover	113
Tip 20: Ask Open-Ended Questions	119
Tip 21: Nontechnical Questions	125
Tip 22: What *Not* to Ask	129
Tip 23: Who Else Should Interview a Candidate?	133
Tip 24: Value of Certification	137
Tip 25: Value of Commitment	143
Tip 26: Value of Education	147
Tip 27: Take Notes *During* the Interview	153
Tip 28: Offering the Correct Amount for an IT Position	157
Tip 29: Other Ideas Besides More Money	161
Tip 30: Have a "D-IQ" (Developer IQ)	167
Tip 31: Things to Watch Out For	173
Tip 32: Watch Out for the New Guy Who Can't Code	179
Tip 33: When and How to *Stop* an Interview	183
Tip 34: Common Hiring Mistakes	187

Tip 35: It Might Not Go Well Anyway   **191**

Tip 36: Close It Down   **195**

Section C: Hirin'

Tip 37: Checking References   **201**

Tip 38: Hire Like Your Gonna Have to Eventually Fire 'Em   **205**

Tip 39: Don't be Afraid to make 'Em Dance   **209**

Tip 40: Hiring in Boom and Bust Times   **215**

Tip 41: Assign Roles to Co-Interviewers   **219**

Tip 42: How Can I Get Better at This?   **221**

Complete List of Key Points

Introduction to Hiring Geeks

Key Points

- Who is this book for?

- Who should buy this book?

- How is this book laid out?

- How is each Tip laid out?

Details

Who is this book for?

- People hiring geeks. "Geeks" is a complimentary term we use for describing computer professionals. They may have 25 minutes of experience (they just got out of college) or they may have 25 years of experience (they have been doing this IT thing for a while).

- Both types have their plusses and minuses, by the way, and we will address those in detail throughout the book. (Specifically, see <u>Tip 5: How to Hire Someone who has More Technical Knowledge Than You</u> and <u>Tip 13: Should Your Hire an Overqualified Candidate?</u>)

- People in charge of hiring for their departments.

- People trying to get hired at any job.

- Founders of technology startups, whether they have a technical background or not.

Who should buy this book?

- You have to *give* an interview. (What should you ask?)

- You have to *go to* an interview. (What should you answer?)

How is this book laid out?

- It has three parts: **Weedin'**, **Interviewin'**, **Hirin'**.

- **Weedin'** discusses the difficult task of sorting through the hundreds of initial resumes. You have to get that number down to a manageable size, and we offer you some concrete tips on how to do that— how to reduce your work and find quality candidates.

- **Interviewin'** discusses how to conduct the most effective—both for you and for the candidate—type of interview. What is the best type of interview? How can you get better? We answer questions like that.

- **Hirin'** discusses how to effectively 'pull the trigger' once you have gone through the weeding and interviewing processes and have found your candidate.

How is each Tip laid out?

- Each one has three parts: **Key Points**, **Details**, and **Real World Stories**.

- **Key Points** give you a quick summary of the tip. The points are just an overview sentence like: "Decide if you need a consultant or an employee *before* you interview."

- **Details** expand on the key points. This section discusses the finer points of the overview. (For the employee/consultant point, for example, there are five sub points.)

- **Real World Stories**. The authors have over 40 years of combined experience in the software industry working with over 30 companies—we know a lot of people and have heard a lot of stories. This section includes stories that apply to that Tip. For example:

Real World Story

I have interviewed geeks and been interviewed—I am a geek. And one thing I know: we're different. We have different skill sets, different ways of presenting those skills sets, different things we want. And non-geeks who interview geeks but don't recognize that difference pay the price. Whether the market for technical talent is expanding or shrinking, if you don't acknowledge that you are in a different interviewing situation, you will cause both you and the candidate harm.

I was in an interview once where the interviewer clearly had no idea about what she was asking. She had been given a list of applications to ask about and she walked through them, pretending to understand what she was asking about.

It took me about 4.5 seconds to understand what was going on. But as I processed her questions—I knew I could fake the answers she was looking for—I started to wonder if I even wanted the job. Did this company really know what they wanted? Or did they just copy the requirements from some other job posting?

I knew that some of the tools she was asking about were fairly obscure, but I also knew that I was not talking to a person I was going to work with.

Ultimately, I answered every question truthfully, sometimes explaining to her slowly (so she could write it down) why I did not have the particular skills she asked about.

I eventually got the job offer, loved the job, and never saw that person again. But it was a close call—for both me and the company.

- *Programmer, 28*

Why You Have to Do This

Key Points

- Why you need to hire.

- Why you have to be involved in hiring.

- Who do you want to work next to/with?

- Being involved in hiring affects "Big Picture" stuff for you.

- Hire the best resource not only for right this minute, but also for the future.

- Your team has strengths and weaknesses.

- You may be starting a team from scratch, backfilling a position or hiring for a new position due to growth.

Details

Why you need to hire.

- For one thing, if you don't, someone else will. Sounds obvious, but the point is more subtle: don't 'outsource' this critical function. You need to be directly involved in this process because it affects your personal success in a direct way.

- Another bonus is that you can make hiring a chance to fill your team with your people. We don't mean people from your hood, although that happens. We mean people who share your philosophy about how a company should be run, how to work well, and (not trivially) who is in charge. When you see people follow each other from company to company, it is because they have figured out how to work together.

- No need to beat around the bush here: hiring someone means a certain balance of power that occurs between two people. One person is in the driver's seat, one or more people are in the passenger's seat. It takes a while, but eventually most people figure if they want to drive the car or sit next to the driver. Each has its perks, but for the purposes of this book, we discuss the details of 'how to drive' regarding the hiring process.

Why you have to be involved in hiring.

- As much as you may not like to admit it, hiring—and firing—are an integral part of most manager's jobs. There is no point in complaining about it and plenty of reasons to embrace the challenge and make it the opportunity it can be.

- We know, we know, you don't have time. You are very busy. Do we have any idea how busy you are? You are not too busy to be involved in hiring. But do it the right way; do at the right level; do it so it gives you the most bang for the buck.

Who do you want to work next to/with?

- What kind of person do you want to be working with three months from now, one year from now?

- Some people are brilliant coders but not great humans to be around—you may want to hire them anyway, or you may not.

Being involved in hiring affects Big Picture stuff for you.

- You have to hire because your success and the success of the people reporting to you, the product you are creating or service you are providing and the profitability of your company is ultimately determined by your ability to find the right people.

- As the manager (or even as a team lead), you have insights into the structure, relationships, technical abilities and technical gaps better than anyone else in the company does. Putting that knowledge into getting the right teammates is a great use of that knowledge.

Hire the best resource not only for right this minute, but also for the future.

- While you do have an immediate need to fill a position with specific skills in mind, the future is full of change. Not only do you need to hire for what you need today, but you also need to hire for what you will need in six months or the next year. Current skills are important, and a trajectory of acquiring and employing new skills is equally important. You need to balance the present day needs with your anticipated needs in the future.

Your team has strengths and weaknesses.

- You might be producing awesome user interfaces, but your performance is limiting the adoption of your product, or vice versa and you have the back end nailed but your user interface is about as exciting as watching grass grow on a PC from 1990 with a green screen CRT with ASCII art. You know these strengths and weaknesses better than the HR department.

- Before you start reviewing resumes, take a real inventory of your current skills and the components your department is weak using. Sometimes, there are some revelations that may not seem directly tied to the delivery of your projects, but are important to driving future success. For instance, you may have been doing fine with your web delivery and you really want to expand into the Android platform, so you need to jump start your development and hire someone with some experience on Android.

You may be starting a team from scratch, backfilling a position or hiring for a new position due to growth.

- Regardless of your situation, you have to be aware that everyone is going to have to work together. It would not be optimal to have an individual who is dedicated to having complete requirements before a single line of code is written when you know you will be running an agile software development shop who will run in short sprints to help define the requirements. It may be important to you that everyone is comfortable with a specific platform. For instance, perhaps you want someone familiar with Apple and Linux, or maybe you prefer dedicated Windows developers. Maybe you don't care and will provide the most productive platform for each individual. Either way, you don't want any operating system zealots spending time attempting to convert others to their operating system of choice instead of producing a product.

- Balancing your needs today, understanding what weakness you need to correct in your team, and knowing that the new hires will fit together is your responsibility.

Real World Story

Once, I had the responsibility—and opportunity—to build a team from scratch. The company had lost *every* individual in the software development department, and the department had to be rebuilt from the ground up. Additionally, the location of the department was changing; not just to a different floor in the same building, but to a location several states away.

Not only was the location changing, but the philosophy of the software development organization was also changing, too. What had been a philosophy of an occasional release of the product was shifting to a very structured approach with regularly scheduled releases. Additionally, we were inheriting a large code base which was broken, could only be built on a magic machine, and had no build scripts.

The needs were clear: we had to have people who had worked in the technologies in use before and who were either experienced with agile software development methods or weren't at their first county fair. It was a tall order to find the resources with the technical chops, either had experience or wanted to work with agile techniques, and who had experience with working in a large code base. This meant we weren't going bottom fishing for the entry-level people. We had to find people with 10–20 years of experience who had been in huge code bases before—maybe had even stepped into, and straightened out, inherited code. All this had to be in the forefront of our thinking as we entered the hiring process. We knew the skill level we were hiring and we knew the salary range necessary to attract the resources we needed. Additionally, we knew the philosophy the individuals would have to adopt before we even posted the job.

Knowing this ahead of time and being personally involved in the selection of the people to fill the needed jobs led to a successful team that was able to breathe life back into a rotting corpse. It wasn't easy, but soon the direction was turned around and the company became profitable.

• *Development Director, 38*

Section A: Weedin'

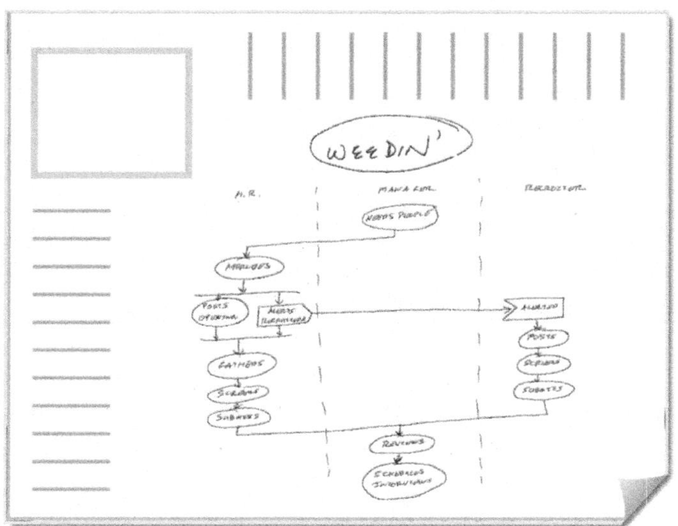

Tip 1: Always be Looking for Superior Talent. Always.

When we say, "always be looking," we mean "always" be looking. Modern corporations—modern organizations of any kind—are always hiring and always firing. Get used to it.

As a manager and a potential hirer, you should shift your attitude from "I need to fill the senior Java programmer position by the end of the month" to "I am always on the lookout for superior talent. I am not technically hiring right now, and even though we are at our children's soccer game, send me your resume to this email address."

Key Points

- The right person suddenly appears at the "wrong" time.

- Projects seldom go as planned.

- Life seldom goes as planned.

- Hiring is like dating.

- Keep an eye out for out-of-the-box talent.

- Always.

Details

The right person suddenly appears at the "wrong" time.

- Sometimes you know exactly what kind of talent you need, but other times you had no idea you needed a specific talent until it popped up in front of you.

Projects seldom go as planned.

- Most technical projects; most development projects; most projects in general seldom go according to plan. You may have a carefully constructed project plan in May to finish by October with six people working 40 hours a week, but we both know that that plan can quickly morph into an actual adventure; one that requires eight people to work 60 hours a week just to finish before Christmas. If you are looking for talent early in the project, you won't be forced to scramble later.

Life seldom goes as planned.

- Classically, you can often find things in life when you don't need them. If you keep a copy of the resume or store the contact info in a place you can find it later, you will increase your "Hiring Happiness Quotient."

Hiring is like dating.

- The right person may come along when you least expect it. Be prepared to act, and to act quickly.

Specifically keep an eye out for out-of-the-box talent.

- Some skills—people looking to learn how to program, for example—can be found under every rock. But a lot of technical talent is much harder to find; it can be a very specialized item. "Always be looking" means making that contact possibly work later.

Always.

- Yep, we said "always." Good technical talent is hard to find. It is even harder to find when you are looking for it; which is why you should always be looking. Even if you already have a full team of good DBAs, for example, if you spot someone who looks brilliant, our advice is to bring them in and talk to them. Face-to-face may convince you that he/she is not as brilliant as you thought; or they may not be available for three months; or they maybe they haven't showered for a year. In any case, you should always be looking.

Real World Story

I network all the time looking for new employees, but one of the best sources is the existing employees. When they bring me a resume and can talk up that person, I know that there is a good chance that the referral would be a good fit. The employee knows the person whose resume they brought to me and they were impressed with the person before. That's reason enough to contact the referral.

More than once, I've gotten a referral that wasn't even for the department the employee worked for. It's pretty amazing when a network administrator brings in a resume for a customer support person who actually impressed them—that's talent. That happened to me once where we didn't have an opening at that moment but we knew we would in a couple of months. The candidate was great, and we hired her. She ended up being with the company for over six years and ended up managing the QA department. We would have missed that benefit had we simply said, "We don't have an opening right now."

- *Customer Support Manager, 45*

Tip 2: Talk to HR—or Not

Key Points

- Some companies have HR departments, some don't.

- Some companies have *very capable* HR people, some don't.

- If you have an active, useful HR department, here's why you *should* use them:

- If you have an inactive or useless HR department, here's why you should *avoid* them:

Details

Some companies have HR departments, some don't.

- Many small companies haven't "gotten around" to setting up an HR department. HR people are seldom early hires in a startup, although many companies have come to realize that people, not only software, hardware, or IP, can be their ticket to continued success.

Some companies have *very capable* HR people, some don't.

- It is not hard to find someone from a large company to tell you their "HR horror stories." Because it is a service position, though, a lot of its work is invisible. Brilliant HR decisions might be being made behind your back—a brilliant health benefits broker might have been chosen, for example—but you're not going to know that.

If you have an active, useful HR department, here's why you should *use* them:

- One of the biggest challenges in hiring these days is moving from 500 resumes received to 10 resumes to look at seriously. This is hard work and work you should offload to someone else. After all, they don't have to know Java to be able to tell if someone has over ten years of Java experience.

If you have an inactive, useless HR department, here's why you should *avoid* them:

- For one thing, they can cause you more effort and time than they can save you. They are supposed to be making things streamlined for you, not adding another step to the process. If you want to, and your company is small enough—some companies are fine with this, but some are not—run the entire process yourself and inform them at the end. ("There is a new programmer starting in two weeks. She'll need a laptop, a cube with the development team on the third floor, and her starting salary will be $65,000.")

- For another, sometimes your requirements might be too technical for non-technical people to understand. Determining how many years of programming a developer has is not hard, but evaluating if "low level coding" counts as "comparable experience" for your position can be hard. And sometimes only a very technically qualified person can do it.

Real World Story

I've been on both sides of a good and bad HR department. The bad HR barely was able to collate resumes after printing them out. It was a running joke that if the benefits and 401(k) weren't outsourced, we wouldn't have had any.

On the other hand, I worked for a company that had an HR department that was on its game. They negotiated with recruiters, weeded resumes, explained benefits, handled all the paperwork, and helped sell working for the company. This department was so on top of things that when we had a great candidate, they could get an offer letter to them before the interview visit was complete. I could send the candidate home with an offer letter in hand—a very powerful capability

that closed the deal the next morning in all but a
couple of cases.

• *Manager of Software Development, 29*

Tip 3: How to Get Help with Your Hiring

Key Points

- How much help you get depends on the stage your company is in.

- Ask for help—your company has people to do this.

- Use your existing staff.

Details

How much help you get depends on the stage your company is in.

- Depending on what stage your company is currently in, you may or may not have additional people to help. In the bare bones, two-guys-in-a-garage stage, there isn't anyone else, and unless you have some angel investor, you don't have the cash to pay someone to help weed through responses to a job posting or to help you interview. In this situation, you're stuck.

- Later stage start-ups and larger companies will have an HR department. Use them to screen the resumes if you're hiring directly and to be present during part of the interview to explain benefits and all the "administrivia" so you can focus on the technical aspects of the interview.

- In between, you still should get help. Recruiters can outsource some of the work for you. Don't expect the first set of resumes you get from a recruiter to be a perfect fit; the recruiter needs to understand what you want and it is your responsibility to tell them. Don't be afraid to look into using smaller recruiting companies—they are hungry. Yes, you'll need to pay them, but let them do the screening and read through all the resumes. Your time needs to be spent for the company you work for, and this is a way to multiply the force applied to the problem.

Ask for help—your company has people to do this.

- If you're in the trenches of IT or software development, it might be easy to cop an attitude and wonder: "What does HR do all day?" After the benefits are set up, the 401(k) program is in place, besides doing paperwork for hiring and firing, most managers who are developing or working with products honestly have no clue what an HR person does. They can do a lot and it's your responsibility to use them.

- Get HR to screen the resumes in response to your job postings. Have them handle the benefit questions. Have HR do the background checks.

Use your existing staff.

- Head off any future complaining regarding not being involved in the decisions of the department by leveraging your existing employees. Have the employees you currently have help screen resumes. If they haven't done this task before, coach them in what you are looking for in a resume by explaining to them what kind of skills say "Buy Me" in a resume.

- At least a portion of the interview can, and should, be performed by the people you have. They will have to work with the "newbie" and involving them in the interview itself (and listening to their feedback) will help transition the new hire and the existing people into a working relationship.

Real World Story

A Near Disaster

I was used to going it alone, writing job descriptions, screening resumes, making initial contacts, setting up the interview, interviewing. Only at that point would I contact HR, and only then to have them put together an offer letter.

Suddenly, we had a new HR department and things were going to change and change quickly. Now HR would make contacts, screen, schedule the interview, and—wonder of wonders—do a background check. All of this looked like control being pulled away and felt like it would reduce my ability to hire someone and get work done! It all seemed wasteful, and it would not be excessive to say I wasn't pleased.

But one incident changed my perspective.

I had identified a candidate and passed them back to HR to do all the administration stuff, including the background check. The candidate was perfect, said all the right things, seemed to have all the skills that we needed; I just wanted HR to hurry up and hire them already.

Then my phone rang. It was the new HR folks. Not good news: I couldn't hire the guy. Of course, I asked why not. After all, I had just gone through a week of interviewing and needed another developer. I asked for details and HR wouldn't say, just that it was not a good idea to hire the guy. A few weeks later, I'm watching the evening news and the guy is going to jail for attempting to murder his wife.

HR saved me a bunch of trouble and now, as The Monkees sang, "I'm a Believer."

- *Development Team Lead, 30*

Tip 4: Internal Hires

Key Points

- Sometimes the stars you are looking for work for your own company—but in an entirely different division/section/building/country.

- Check them out first without a lot of hassle.

- Some managers have been known to read internal forums and sounding boards inside their companies to see how potential internal employees act.

Details

Sometimes the stars you are looking for work for your own company...

- …but in an entirely different division/section/building/country.

- Posting the job internally first has all kinds of benefits (see Tip 2: Talk to HR—or Not), and one of them is that someone may have done all of the initial legwork for you. If they already work for the company, they have laptops, logins, etc..

- These candidates have a leg up on outside competition. They know the business of the company and should be able to pull from that experience in the new position.

Check them out first without a lot of hassle.

- You don't *have* to hire them, but if they are even close to your qualifications, you should at least bring them in for an interview. They might be just the right person.

- This action also provides a story over the long haul: your company will promote from within and provides a career path. Typically, geeks have to jump to a new company to get promoted. Retain the talent you have.

Some managers have been known to read internal forums and sounding boards inside their companies to see how potential internal employees act.

- If they often, in these forums, are yelling about small issues, they shouldn't be asked for an interview.

- It's also worth searching on the Internet. Have they posted anything derogatory about the company? What's going on in their LinkedIn profile/Facebook page?

Real World Story

Raw talent sometimes magically appears at your door. The kid straight from college looking for his/her first chance to prove his or herself is opportunity loudly knocking on the door. While I've hired many people for their first job with software development, one in particular stands out from the rest. When we first interviewed, she wasn't completely qualified for the position we were hiring for, as her studies were a little different, but there was a great positive attitude. She ended up going through the interview undeterred. As luck would have it, we had another position for an entry level QA person that would get her onboard with the company. It was a gamble on both sides, maybe she'd wash out or maybe she'd become a superstar. Thankfully, it was the latter.

In a year, we could get a junior software developer on the team, and since she already knew the product, we encouraged her to apply. She did apply, and of course knew what to say in the interview, so we moved her to the developer position. She jumped into the maintenance of a product that would soon be retired, but was still in daily use for paying customers. Never a complaint, even when the days turned into extra hours and some weekend support duties. The company did invest in some training, and training just happened by doing the job.

After nearly 18 months, the product was retired and she was moved to another product development team. The company got an extremely loyal employee who knew the business and was rapidly picking up the finer points of software development such as design patterns and new programming languages.

While the experience did not exist on the first day, she grew into the role and the company never had to teach her to un-learn habits and approaches that wouldn't fit the business model.

It look a while to "get" the contributions that a senior person might have been able to provide in a shorter time, but during her training, she learned more about what the company really did, it's strengths and weakness, than some senior executives. Eventually, she was promoted to be the senior resource and even had some team lead responsibilities. None of this would have been possible if we'd passed on her from the first interview.

- *Director, Software Development, 38*

Tip 5: How to Hire Someone Who Has More Technical Knowledge than You

Key Points

- Let them explain the technology to you.

- Don't try and fake it.

- Ask them how difficult it was to acquire/learn this technology.

- If it was easily done, that might be a good sign the person can learn new things.

- If it was difficult to do, it might be a sign the person does not yet fully grasp the technology.

Details

Let them explain the technology to you.

- If they have mastery of a subject, they should be able to describe it, or better yet, teach it. It's OK to ask questions for the candidate to back up and fill in some background before proceeding.

- Get them up at a white board to draw pictures; they really are often worth thousands of words and you have limited time to interview.

- As a side benefit, you'll get to see their presentation style. Can they communicate clearly? Are they pitching to the right level for the audience?

Don't try and fake it.

- Today's technologies are complex and someone trying to fake it is often easily uncovered.

- You should be prepared enough to know a little about the person and the technologies they are highlighting on their resume before the interview. This preparation can lead to good questions to use during the interview.

Ask them how difficult it was to acquire/learn this technology.

- Ask them how they picked up the skills. Were they sent to a training class, or did they find a whisper of a hint of an idea and track it down themselves?

- Before the discussion is over, relate the technology or skill to their present job. How did learning that skill help the company? How would they measure the ROI of the time spent to learning the technology?

If learning this technology was easily done...

- …that might be a good sign the person can learn new things.

If they say learning this technology was difficult to do...

- …it might be a sign the person does not yet fully grasp the technology.

Real World Story

As a young manager, I had to hire someone to continue development on the code generation portion of our product. This wasn't generating source code to be complied later, but generating the machine instructions dynamically in memory; basically a compiler inside of a product that generated code for the more static portions of the product to invoke on the fly.

We had someone who had worked on this section for years, and he had decided to move on and leave the industry entirely. It was a huge hole to fill in the software development department and an enormous hole in the company. If not filled correctly, it would severely impact the ability of the company to deliver product. It was a bad situation and it was made worse by the fact that there was no way I could dial a recruiter and say, "Give me 10 resumes with this skill set." To further complicate things, I had tangential experience myself with the work, but I hadn't directly worked on the code and it was always a black box to the rest of the development staff.

So here I was hunting for candidates, in a skill that I had scant knowledge, and trying to screen the applicants. The easy part was that there were maybe five candidates who could even attempt to meet the requirements for the job.

One candidate was very appealing right from the resume, as he had done the type of work we needed in the past and was local. It was just dumb luck that I found someone in the same city, and the stars must have aligned because he worked in the building next door! I did the phone interview one morning, and when I found out he was next door, I offered to meet in the park between the buildings in a few minutes. He agreed, and our first meeting was in that park.

We shook hands, and I knew instantly the guy was twice my age. With his experience, he could have easily snowed me. But I had an ace in the hole in the situation: the leading question. I knew enough about the problem space to phrase the question and keep the conversation going—and I also knew to shut up. I was the hiring manager, and regardless of his experience, he needed me to make a job offer. We discussed the company, and a little about the product and what skills I was looking for and then I set up a leading question and let him talk.

He explained similar work he had done in the past and what the application was as I listened and nodded at the right times, and then the spark happened: he started asking me questions. Not general questions about the 401(k) benefits, but detailed stuff like a common problem, the possible solutions, and which approach did we take. Since my experience developing the product was using the output of the generator, we could start talking about the interface between the selections of code, what the stack looked like, what was the order of parameters, and so forth. I may not have known every intricate detail of the work that he would do, but I knew how to use the output and how to interface with the code he would continue to enhance and create.

The secret here wasn't that I knew every detail, but working it to the interface points where we both were comfortable. I shut up to let him talk, only asking more leading questions and putting his responses through the B.S. filter in my head as fast as he was talking. The filter never lit up, and I ended up making him an offer (after interviewing a few more candidates).

- *IT Manager, 32*

Tip 6: Consultant or Employee?

Key Points

- Decide if you need a consultant or an employee *before* you interview.

- Real quick definitions.

- The line is blurry between consultant and employee.

- If you're in doubt if the position is an employee or a contractor, fall back to thinking how long the job will last.

- Here's a real example where a consultant is extremely useful.

Details

Decide if you need a consultant or an employee *before* you interview.

- The personalities for both are different, and how you treat them varies.

- If you need a quick hit, someone to get in, get the job done and get out, then go the consultant route.

- If you need someone who will stay with the company for years and grow, then you should hire an employee.

- Put bluntly, consultants are temporary fill-ins who need to deliver on a schedule without being coddled; and if they can't deliver, then get rid of them. Employees should be treated with more respect because you want someone who knows the details of your business and can make long-term decisions.

- The problem is most software developers don't think about your business and really want to "write cool code." Finding a software developer that bridges the gap is difficult and rare.

Real quick definitions.

- *Employee* is a fulltime worker that is paid by and works for a company. Generally, they put in 40 hours a week, although many put in more hours and some put in fewer hours. Employees receive fulltime pay (generally a salary, but it can be an hourly wage) and benefits such as health insurance.

- *Consultants* are not fulltime workers, they do not work for your company, and they do not receive benefits from you. They generally work only the hours you want them to work and that number can vary from one hour to over 60. You can hire them or fire them at will.

- However, these are only very general definitions. In the old days (30 years ago), that line was clear. Now there are "consultants" working for other companies, employees doing freelance on the side, etc.. There are many variations.

The line is blurry between consultant and employee.

- You may want to hire someone on a trial basis and convert him or her to an employee if it's working out for both of you. These individuals may have the title of "consultant" temporarily.

- In other cases, you have to be very careful how to treat real consultants. If you don't you may land in a legal battle, as illustrated in 2000 by the "permatemp" suit that Microsoft had to deal with. In that case, Microsoft tried to get around paying benefits by terming the employees "independent contractors." Be very careful with the terminology you use for your employees. Given the entitlement mentality of the early 21st century society where everyone is a victim (for simply being employed!), you may end up in court. If you have any questions about the title, consult with your HR department to get the current details for your locale.

If you're in doubt if the position is an employee or a contractor...

- ...fall back to thinking how long the job will last.

- If you envision the work lasting for a few weeks or months and then you won't have further work for that person, you need a consultant. If the need is continual and ongoing, you need an employee.

- With the confusion of the word "consultant" and its misapplication by recruiters, it may be tempting to call an employee a consultant but don't be tricked into this lazy mode of thinking.

- Cut out the B.S. and decide upfront what you need and both you and the employee will be much happier for it.

Here's a real example where a consultant is extremely useful.

- User Interface design for a new product or enhancement on your existing product.

- You may have someone on your staff that produces the user interfaces for your product; it's been their job for a long time and you're generally happy with their work. That's all fine, but with the opportunity to build a new product/module/enhancement it may be time to shake things up a bit and challenge the status quo. An injection of fresh blood can give the effort a needed boost, and competition always strengthens the product. Set up some competition, and using a consultant who will not be involved with the company in a few months is perfect. To put it another way, trees grow new, strong branches after weathering a storm.

Real World Story

In 1996, Microsoft was charged with a class action lawsuit by employees who had a status of "temporary" or "freelance." These employees didn't get to participate in the stock purchase plan, but they had such a long tenure with Microsoft that they worked like "regular" employees. The line was very blurry.

The lawsuit ended up ruling in favor of the employees, and Microsoft owed millions.

Microsoft lost this battle for not converting temporary or freelance workers, and they have a lot more money and lawyers than the average company does. The moral is: be very careful with this issue.

- *http://en.wikipedia.org/wiki/Permatemp#Vizcaino_v._Microsoft*

Tip 7: Write Down a Job Description

Key Points

- Even if you are a very, very experienced manager that has hired hundreds of people, you should scribble down a job description for the position you are trying to fill.

- There are many reasons a formal job description is useful.

- Often HR can either start the process or even do this for you.

- You've seen plenty of job descriptions yourself, including those times when you were looking for a job yourself!

Details

Even if you are an experienced manager that has hired hundreds of people...

- …you should scribble down a job description for the position you are trying to fill.

- In fact, it is a good idea for everyone in the company to have a relatively formal job description—but you and I know that probably is not going to happen. The best we can hope for is to describe what the poor new sap is supposed to do.

There are many reasons a formal job description is useful. Among them are:

- Items in the description provide a template for requirements you can give HR

- Items in the description provide a template for questions you can ask the candidate

- You have a clear picture of the expectations for the job, and something to base a performance review upon when the time comes.

Often HR can either start the process or even do this for you.

- Even in the turbulent IT industry, where yesterday's Java developer is today's mobile app designer, there is some uniformity of positions.

- In many companies, for example, you can't just make up this stuff yourself—the job description needs to meet certain legal requirements.

- Even if you have all kinds of latitude, you can get HR to give you some generic descriptions for positions that you can then modify. You may think you have needs no one else has ever thought of, but you probably don't. Get help with this if you can.

You've seen plenty of job descriptions yourself.

- As someone in charge of hiring new employees, you have probably seen a lot of job descriptions out there—including those times when you were looking for a job yourself!

- One of the features we have always noticed is that the job descriptions are often long laundry lists of requirements. ("Candidates must have written their own emulators, managed development teams of 20 people or more, and have 35 years of hands-on coding in their background." What B.S.! Nobody meets all those requirements, and the hiring manager clearly does not know how to write a job description.)

- Those laundry lists of requirements may provide a reason to reject a candidate without saying, "We just didn't like you," but they may also stop the next rock star from applying to your company.

Make sure you address the following issues:

- Job title; Position summary; Immediate supervisor; Number of direct reports (if any); Minimum and/or specific experience requirements; Education; Training and Certification requirements (if any); Travel (if any); Salary (if any).

- (Just kidding on that last one…)

Real World Story

It's been said that you can't improve anything unless you can measure it. And while a job description is not a 100% objective measurement, it does provide a soft yardstick to help guide your efforts. The act of writing something down on paper (or the electronic representation of paper) helps you see what is in your head. When you see what you have written, you can work to improve not only the writing, but also the thought process that brought out the writing.

For the first couple of rounds of hiring, I did not see the value in writing a job description. My immature thought process was that I'd somehow know talent when I saw it in the interview. My naivety led to some missteps, and I ended up hiring a few employees who were not a fit for the company, technology-wise or culturally.

After being pushed by a recruiter for a job description, I finally started writing one down. It took a while, and my first attempts followed the form of other job descriptions I found online that seemed similar to what we were looking for in skill sets and experience. After a few drafts, I had a description that mirrored the successful individual contributors.

The revelation in this process was that I was finally able to put my finger on why some employees were not successful. Not only did this effort pay dividends in hiring the next round of developers, but it also uncovered and named some problems that as a manager, I could work to fix and improve in the current staff.

Once complete, the quality of the resumes I
received from the recruiters improved dramatically.
Instead of 10 interviews to find one candidate who
might be a fit, we were finding a candidate in three
interviews and having a hard time deciding which
one we should hire! A little investment went a long
way in reducing the time to fill a position and took
less time away from the work we should have
been producing for our company.

- *Software Development Manager, 28*

Tip 8: Using Social Networking

Key Points

- Look on Craigslist!

- Look on Facebook… duh.

- Look on LinkedIn.

- Check MeetUp.

- Host hacker face-offs.

- Google the job/person/industry

Details

Look on Craigslist!

- It may sound strange to use Craigslist as a hiring tool, but in fact, it is a widely used networking tool. A quick glance at your city's "Jobs" section will show you how many companies (possibly even your competitors) are using the service.

- A major misconception about Craigslist jobs is that they only offer low-level, service jobs. Those jobs exist, of course, but there are a lot more employment offers on that site. Recent listings for our local Craigslist included: "Senior Rails Developer," "Web Application Developers (Ruby, Python, PHP)," "PHP RESTful Web Services Engineer," and "Senior Drupal Developer."

- Take a look—you'll see listings like "Senior Linux Systems Engineer (Expert Level)," and "Google Data Center Opportunities." Are these the kinds of jobs you are interviewing for? Then why aren't you listing them on Craigslist?

- One of the reasons Craigslist is so popular, of course, is its price. Listing the jobs on the site is nominal, sometimes $25 or less— hard to beat that price. (Not that you care, but Craigslist is often blamed for the demise of many newspapers around the country. Revenue from job and car sales listings made a up significant portion of many papers' income.)

Look on Facebook... duh.

- Many, many humans (850 million, according to Mark Zuckerberg's 2011 numbers) are on Facebook. See what there is about a candidate you are thinking of hiring.

- If they post damaging information on there, they deserve the pain they cost themselves. Many potential hiring companies first Google and then look up their candidates on Facebook.

- Be careful not to eliminate a candidate for 'politically incorrect' reasons. If they are a devoted fan of a football team that competes with your favorite team, or they vacation often in a city you hate, for example, ignore this kind of data. Focus on issues that relate to their professional careers. If they spout off about how proud they are to have missed deadlines without paying any consequences, for example, you should be worried.

Look on LinkedIn.

- If a candidate is not on LinkedIn these days, either they have had the same job for 20 years or they have a poor understanding of how hiring happens in the very competitive IT environment we work in.

- Not only should *your* resume be on there, but your next hire's should be on there, too.

- Note that you can easily see who has viewed your LinkedIn profile. This may be a non-issue for you, or it may be a critical piece of data you do not want revealed.

Check MeetUp.

- A recent MeetUp listing was for "Mobile Application Development with Flex and ColdFusion." (Okay, it was held in London, but still…)

- Another recent MeetUp was for "Ruby on Rails 3"—and that one was in Massachusetts.

- Don't worry; you probably won't be the only hiring manager there. Some meetings have tables where companies can set up informal hiring 'booths.'

Host hacker face-offs.

- These are not easy to set up but they can very, very valuable.

- Think about sponsoring a night at one of the local user groups. You may pick up candidates for the cost of a couple of pizzas.

Google the job/person/industry

- Use Bing or Google, or whichever search tool you prefer, but go out into the big, scary online world and find out about jobs like yours in your area. You should know this.

Real World Story

If you want to see an example of a hacker's faceoff, see the movie *The Social Network*. In the film, Mark Zuckerberg, the founder of Facebook, sets up an intense, on-site competition between developers to help him determine who is best qualified to work under the pressure the job brings.

Because the jobs are with a company that (at the time) was operated on a college campus, there was a large amount of alcohol consumption required while the coding challenge was happening… you do not need to duplicate that aspect.

Even xkcd has parodied the relationship between
a little drinking and "programming skill":
http://xkcd.com/323/ (the webcomic's infamous
"Ballmer Peak" episode.)

- *IT Manager, 42*

Tip 9: Network Your A** Off

You've heard it a million times—the best way to find a job is through your network. That is certainly not *always* true, but it is true a lot of the time. And by "your network," we don't *only* mean your electronic network—although we do mean that, too. (See the previous <u>Tip 8: Using Social Networks</u>).

Key Points

- The candidate has probably used their networks to find this interview.

- You should use your own network to find the right candidate.

- Previous co-workers are a great source of job information.

- Other places to look include…

Details

While talking to the candidate, keep in mind that he/she probably used their networks to find this interview.

- Most candidates now know that companies get hundreds of responses to every job they post, and in many ways, whether they find a job—never mind the perfect job, just *any* job—is a numbers game.

- They are better served working through someone they know.

You should use your own network to find the right candidate.

- Do you attend user groups? Put out the word. Do you frequent particular forums? (No, not those forums; the other kind.) Some forums don't want you posting jobs, 'looking for position X,' etc. But that does not mean you cannot lurk around, notice particular posters, and possibly contact them. This sounds suspiciously like stalking, but what we are saying here is that you should always be looking for talent that fits your specific technical needs.

- When we say, "always looking," we mean, "*always* looking." (See <u>Tip 1: Always be Looking for Superior Talent. Always.</u>)

Previous co-workers are a great source of job information.

- In the small but ever-expanding world that is IT, people often migrate from one technical environment to another, not really caring about the industry or the application, but focusing much more on the development environment.

- Are there interesting coding challenges to be had? Does the whole project look interesting—are they trying something that has not been done before? Your job as a hiring manager is to keep your network alive and mine that network for talent when the need arises.

Other places to look include...

- Members of your department may know of people looking for jobs within your company. (See <u>Tip 4: Internal Hires</u> on hiring internal candidates.)

- Tech meetings

- Colleges and universities in your area that might offer internships

Real World Story

Person-to-person networking that paid off in work:

A fellow IT manager I know got hired through a connection in his church. He was not even looking for a job at the time.

- *IT Manager, 42*

Tip 10: The Good, Bad and Ugly about Using Recruiters

There are plenty of reasons to go ahead and use recruiters, and plenty of reasons not to. Let's review.

Key Points

- Internal recruiters are people who…

- External recruiters are people who…

- Some companies require that you use certain 'recommended' recruiters, or they have 'internal' recruiters.

- Recruiters vary radically in skill. (Duh.)

- Specifically, most recruiters do not have much technical ability.

- External recruiters are generally paid by commission.

- You can certainly use multiple recruiters.

Details

Internal recruiters are people who...

- …work for your company or one of its divisions. They are often part of the HR division.

External recruiters are people who...

- ...work outside the company and may work for a national chain or, less commonly these days, work on their own.

Some companies *require* that you use certain 'recommended' recruiters, or they have 'internal' recruiters.

- If your organization has these, know that it will take a lot of extra work on your part to go *around* these requirements. It is sometimes possible, but generally not suggested. Showing up to HR with a candidate from a 'non-recommended' recruiter can cause you 3.75 pounds of additional paperwork. Just saying.

Recruiters vary radically in skill. (Duh.)

- Some recruiters are *brilliant* at what they do and make a huge difference in a company's success.

- Some recruiters are *terrible* at what they do and make a huge difference in a company's success.

- How can you tell the difference?

- For one thing, each company has its own culture, its own feel, and its own way of doing things. A good recruiter figures out pretty quickly what your company's specific culture is and finds candidates that he/she thinks will work in that world. Not everyone belongs everywhere, and not every geek belongs in every environment, even if the requirement says, "Must be a geek."

Specifically, most recruiters do not have much technical ability.

- IT is complicated enough for most of the people *in* that world, but it is beyond the skills of most people *outside* that world.

- If you find one that can understand your requirements, hang on to them.

- If you cannot find one who can grok what you really need, find the one you think listens the best and work with them. Remember, you are working in a world that is complex, rapidly changing, and full of big risks and big rewards. It is no accident that some people find that world intoxicating, even if they don't understand most of what is going on around them.

External recruiters are generally paid by commission.

- Most external recruiters get between a quarter and a fifth of the candidate's first year salary—once that candidate has been with the company a specified amount of time (typically three months). Those numbers are negotiable, particular in times where hiring managers can find talent in a wide range of places.

- Because external recruiters are often paid by commission, it is in your best interest to treat them as commissioned sales people—their goal is to make a sale, and they are willing to do certain things to make that sale. Of course, the good ones will do those things that make you happiest, in the short *and* long term. Remember that.

You can certainly use multiple recruiters.

- Exclusive arrangements—while they do exist—are rare. More often, a hiring manager will use multiple companies for his/her talent search. The time stamp on the email or the fax machine ends up being the arbiter if two companies submit the same candidate.

- But using multiple recruiters is not the core issue, finding the right recruiter is. Once you find a recruiter/recruiting company that understands your system and your needs, hang on to them.

Real World Story

I've learned that a good recruiter is hard to find. If you have one who knows what your company is about and is able to find and filter candidates well, make sure you keep them. If you're getting deluged with marginal candidates, you need to move on and find a different recruiter (or recruiting firm).

We once attempted to bring in a third recruiting firm after several years of dealing with just two large firms. The new group was billing themselves as a "boutique" recruitment firm who would find the specialty skills and "only bring the best candidates." I'd heard this before at previous jobs, and prepared for a rough ride.

Sure enough, my mailbox was quickly filled in less than 48 hours with candidates who "had exactly what we were looking for" and who were "great guys" with "positive attitudes." To make matters worse, the team that was sending the resumes was not the people we talked to originally. Something was lost in the translation.

Then it got worse. We found someone in the quagmire of resumes they forwarded that would be a good fit. Somehow, they started a bait and switch; the rates, conditions, and terms we had agreed upon were now on a document that was "lost," and the prices were much higher than our original agreement. We had lunch (recruiters love lunch) to discuss it, but nothing changed. We ended the relationship.

We couldn't go forward with the candidate we wanted to hire; he was screwed out of a job, and my company wasted weeks going back and forth, and in the end, produced nothing.

- *Development Manager, 40*

Tip 11: How to Read a Resume

Key Points

- Check the spelling.

- Check out their work history.

- Look at the data.

- What to do about gaps.

- Do the factual claims seem valid?

Details

Check the spelling.

- You don't need to run a spell-checker—that is the candidate's job. But almost all resumes are sent electronically now and running a spell check should be in the "How to Write a Resume 101" class the candidate took. If that candidate has a spelling error in his/her initial presentation to you (his/her resume), that is not a good sign. Most technical jobs—not all, but most—require careful attention to detail.

- If you find a spelling error, do not immediately disqualify the candidate. They may have skills that justify your continued examination. They might, but they might not.

- In these days of hiring managers getting between 300 and 500 resumes per position, candidates have to be super-careful not to self *de-select*. Getting selected is hard enough.

- If you decide to bring the person in for an interview, bring the error up in the interview. See how they react. They may argue that is not an error; they may blush; they may apologize. Take note of how they deal with a small but important problem.

Check out their work history.

- Do they have concrete experience in the area you are hiring for?

- Note that while technical positions seldom require great presentation skills (so a resume from a geek may not be beautiful or attractive), it should be very clear about its subject. There are plenty of places now to get one's resume polished—and by that, we do not mean, "Use the right font." By that, we mean, "Show this person's real skills cleanly."

Look at the data.

- This is something you probably do all the time, so you should be used to it. :-)

- Does the resume just contain a long list of technologies they used? Do you really care about the fact that they worked with CICS back in the '80s? Maybe you do. (There are still a lot of COBOL programs running, for example, and it was introduced decades ago.) But more likely you are interested not only in *what* they have used recently, but also *how* they have used it. If they only present a list with no accompanying text about their own experience with the items on the list, they may be presenting very shallow data.

What to do about gaps.

- Some companies call it "Gap Analysis." No need to panic that there are gaps; many people these days have periods of "consulting." Ask the candidate about it directly and see how they react. If they say, "What gap?" or dissemble or try and fake it, you know how they handle a tough situation. If they say, "I tried this…, I worked on that…, I took classes in this…," etc., that is a good answer. They tried to make the best of a tough situation.

Do the factual claims seem valid?

- This is not as ridiculous a statement as it sounds. Not only do a lot of people lie on their resumes, they often lie *badly*. (See Yahoo's adventures with this issue in 2012 for a huge and startling example.) They claim to have used a language for seven years when you know it has only been around for five, for example. Or they claim to be a senior DBA in the "Executive Summary" section of their resume but their entire job history shows no relevant database background. Or they say they have a PhD from MIT; they might, but then again, they might not.

- Checking claims can sometimes be a simple as doing a search on the Web. Again, save your energy—don't even bother checking factual claims until you have narrowed the potential list down to ten resumes or less. And you don't need to check every claim, of course; just flag anything that stands out.

- Larger companies have entire departments—often called "Human Resources"—that do fact checking, background checking, drug test administering, etc. for you. But smaller companies often do not have the luxury of having someone else do this, so do it smartly.

Real World Story

I went into an interview once where the interviewers told me there was an error in my resume. I was shocked that it was there and shocked that they pointed it out to me. Why was I still in the pool of potential candidates? I wondered.

It turns out their idea of an "error" and mine were quite different: they thought my use of commas was wrong. While they acknowledged that their interpretation might be an 'alternative' one, it still caused me to lose my breath for a second.

Then they proceeded to tell me how many
resumes they found with 'real' spelling errors.
They claimed over half of the resumes they
received contained spelling or grammatical
mistakes. Over half!

- *Jr. Project Manager, 45*

Tip 12: Narrowing Down the List (Initial Step)

Most companies now receive many, many resumes for every job they post. You know the drill, you post a job on a site and then sit back and wait for the torrent to start. Depending on the location and the vagueness of the description, you could be looking at trying to make your way through hundreds if not thousands of resumes.

Key Points

- No one can do this easily. Luckily, it is probably not your job to do it anyway.

- HR is not doing it manually (or they shouldn't be, anyway).

- If you don't have an HR department, you need to find help.

- Toss all resumes like these:

Details

No one can do this easily. Luckily, it is probably not your job to do it anyway.

- It is someone's job in HR to do this.

And they are not doing it manually (or they shouldn't be, anyway).

- Lots of software exists to automate this process so that they can go from 375 resumes to 50. If you are looking for a Flex developer with 3–5 years of experience, they can eliminate all those resumes with no programming experience, recent college graduates with little work experience, Java developers who would love to learn Flex, out-of-country residents, etc.

If you don't have an HR department, you need to find help.

- You may be too small or don't understand their role, but regardless, know that you need to find help.

- If you can't find help or the software to scan for keywords (or don't want to pay for it), below are some quick guidelines to get the number down to a manageable size.

Toss all resumes that:

- Are from out of state, even if you are willing to pay for relocation—and most companies are not these days. Qualified candidates probably live in your state.

- Contains glaring typos.

- Have no mention of the key word you are looking for. (In the example above, the word "Flex" doesn't appear in the last three jobs.)

- Are not in either Word or pdf format. (These formats are the standard now.)

- Feels the need to tell you their life story. (A resume that is over five pages long, for example, is too long these days.)

- Contains too high credentials (do you *need* someone with a PhD?) or too low (if you are reading this book, you probably need someone who has at least graduated from high school).

- Contains too many jobs or too few jobs.

- The candidate is not in the business you are looking for. (The market is less forgiving these days for people looking to jump from one industry to another. If you are in the software development business, you may not be interested in candidates who have spent their entire careers in manufacturing. And the reverse is true, too, of course.)

Use those guidelines and you can cut the numbers down by over half. You still have a ways to go, but you have made progress.

Real World Story

In the early 1990s, before there was Monster, Dice, and other websites to post job openings, everybody posted jobs in the local newspaper. This was an interesting time because of scandals and news like the ongoing S&L crisis, and many companies were running lean. It seemed like every ad would generate 50 or more resumes by Tuesday morning (with more coming in throughout the week). My company wasn't using a recruiter and didn't have much of an HR staff. That meant that it was the responsibility of the hiring manager to weed through every resume.

I'd take home the stack of resumes on Tuesday night and start sorting. With the additional requirement of giving each rejection a reason, the resumes were read and not just glanced at for key words. Piles appeared on my living room floor in an attempt to sort the resumes. One pile contained the first set to start phone screening, another pile for clear rejects (with the reason), and another pile for a second round of phone screens. On it went.

Rejects were the easiest to sort out. A person that lived two states away, or wasn't a programmer, was easy to remove from consideration. Sometimes, the spelling was so atrocious that I gave up halfway through the cover letter. The job hoppers—six months or less at each position— were thrown out. Sometimes it was easy to reject a resume. Others went into the middle pile, with the resumes that clearly warranted a call going right on top.

After the first pass, selecting which ones to call became progressively harder. Weeding through the "good" resumes was difficult because they may have had very dissimilar experience. It was only after doing this task several times that I began to know which industries or companies would have people with knowledge and skills that would translate to my company. An inventory system, maybe not; financial work, maybe. Even after interviewing people from all kinds of backgrounds, it was still a difficult choice.

Honestly, as random as it was, there were times that I would just flip a coin.

This all forced the necessity of the phone screen. The only time these cold calls to a stranger could be made was after working hours. But when else can you make the call? Hours spent on the phone, letting someone sell me on him or herself and bring them into an interview. After the call, if it sounded good to both the candidate and me, we'd schedule an interview.

At least two nights were spent sorting resumes, more nights calling, and there was still the interview to complete. Without developing techniques to sift through all the paper, I'd have been buried under the work. The ability to read and sort resumes quickly was invaluable.

- *Manager of Software Development, 26*

Tip 13: Should You Hire an Overqualified Candidate?

The answer depends on how experienced a manager you are. If you are just getting your management career off the ground, our recommendation is *not* to hire candidates with significantly more experience than your position requires. If you are a seasoned manager, there are some significant advantages (and disadvantages) to doing this.

Key Points

- These candidates require special attention from their manager.

- For one thing, an over-qualified candidate may just be 'parking it for a little while.'

- Another issue is that some people get bored easily.

- Experienced managers can often head this problem off.

- But be careful if you are not up for this level of challenge.

These candidates require special attention from their manager.

- And special attention might be something you may or may not be able to provide. You get a lot, but you also give up a lot.

For one thing, an over-qualified candidate may just be 'parking it for a little while.'

- He or she may be at your place until something better comes along.

- This may not be all bad—maybe all you need in that position is some skills for a short amount of time.

- But it might be terrible—maybe it took you a long time to get this request approved and the last thing you need is to have someone jump out after only a couple of months.

Another issue is that some people get bored easily.

- A lot of people in the computer industry actually get bored easily. If the candidate you are considering is way over-qualified, they may find working at a position way beneath them to be difficult to do. And they may transfer that frustration over to you, your team, or your company.

Experienced managers can often head this problem off.

- Managers who have seen this issue before can bring the topic up during the interview, for example, or they can assign additional (unofficial) tasks to keep the new person busy.

But be careful if you are not up for this level of challenge.

- If you decide to take it on, it could come back and haunt you. "You get a lot, but also you give up a lot."

Real World Story

My boss wondered whether to hire a senior salesperson. The job had remained empty for months and we were heading right into the prime selling season.

- Me: "I don't get it. Why don't you hire the guy and get it over with? He is a senior guy that we can get for half his regular salary." Our sales team was filled with kids right out of college, and this guy had ten years under his belt.

- Boss: "Well, you are right. He is a senior candidate and has a proven record of doubling sales."

- Me: "Okay. So why don't you hire him then?"

- Boss: "Because, he will double sales but I will also get a call at two a.m. asking me to post bail for him."

My boss was a senior manager and he was telling me that this 'over-qualified' person was going to take senior management skills to handle. He eventually hired the guy. No bail was ever required, but other serious personnel challenges did arise.

- *Sales Representative, 27*

I used to have a boss who referred to his team of 14 mostly senior-level developers as "a bunch of thoroughbreds." He did not mean that solely as a compliment. He constantly complained about the 'special care and feeding' this group required. And by that he meant they needed the latest equipment, demanded the latest software, and insisted on all kinds of perks other members of the company did not enjoy (such as *very* flexible working hours). In exchange for the treatment they received, the team rewarded their boss with state-of-the-art software that put the company way in front in their marketplace.

The point is not that the company achieved this status but *how* they achieved it. Yes, they had 14 high-performing employees, but just as importantly, they had the management skill to maximize that kind of firepower. That may seem easy to do, but it isn't.

- *Senior Java Developer, 46*

Section B: Interviewin'

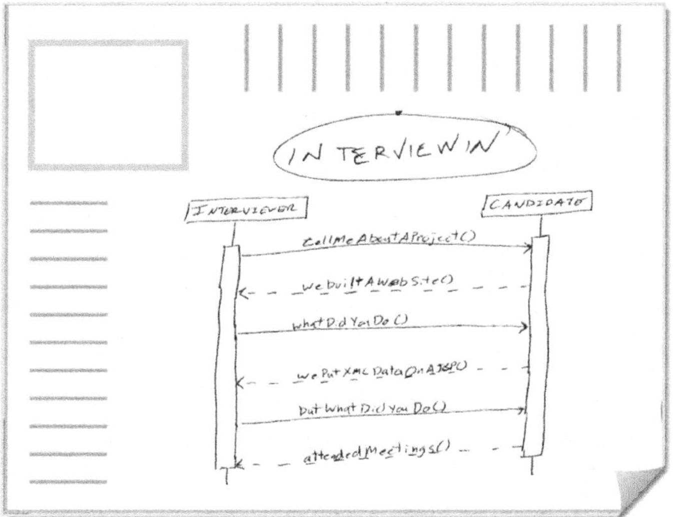

Tip 14: Conduct the Best Type of Interview

The point of great interviews is when the candidate and the company determine as honestly as they can how well they fit together.

Key Points

- When the *candidate* determines, as honestly as they can, how well they fit.

- When the *company* determines, as honestly as they can, how well they fit....

- ...How well they fit together.

- It is fairly common to ask this question directly.

- Just as common is it for them to ask you this question.

- Remember, the perfect interview is when...

- See Tip 33: When and How to *Stop* an Interview on how to bring an interview to an end before it is scheduled to finish.

- See Tip 36: Close It Down on how to finish an interview well.

Details

The point of great interviews is when the candidate and the company determine, as honestly as they can, how well they fit together.

Let's break that phrase apart:

When the *candidate* determines as honestly as they can...

- While some job seekers will take any job they can get, many will not take jobs that are clearly wrong for them. Some will be clear about that during the interview, or very soon afterwards.

When the *company* determines as honestly as they can...

- As the interviewer, your job (during the latter stages of the process) is to briefly present to the candidate what kind of company you work for and what kind of position is available.

- This information may be old news to the interviewee or it may shock them for some reason. (They may say, "Yes, I saw on your website that you have over 50 offices around the world." Or they may say, "Really, I thought you were a local company.") Get that info out now.

...how well they fit together.

- Maybe you need someone more senior but don't have the budget, or maybe they need a job with less travel, but maybe you can both compromise. Or maybe the best idea is to walk away now.

It is fairly common to ask this question directly:

- "If we were to make you an offer—and we are *not* doing so right now, I am just asking a hypothetical question—would you be interested in working for us?"

- Almost everyone is going to say yes.

- But you can sometimes determine by the tone of the person's voice that they do not intend to ever return to this building again, let alone working for your company. Better to find that out now.

- Or they may be genuinely excited at the chance.

Just as common is for them to ask you this question:

- "Given our conversation today, how likely is it that you will offer me a position?"

- Interviewers sometimes say, "Oh, you were great." But they don't always mean it. If you think the interview went poorly or the candidate is not well suited, it is okay to gently send that signal right now. You can say something like "Well, we still have a lot of very qualified candidates to choose among." or "To be honest; we have talked to several candidates who have stronger experience with these technologies." You'll be doing yourself and the candidate a favor if the verdict is clear right away.

Remember, the perfect interview is when...

- …both you and the interviewee find out if you are good match for each other.

- The perfect interview is not if the person is the perfect candidate or your company is the perfect place to work—neither is possible. But it is certainly possible for you to see if the two of you fit well together.

- A simple example: working from home. Some companies encourage it, and some employees absolutely need it. But other employers hate it; some employees even grow to really dislike it. Interviewing a candidate for a position in your organization might mean determining where you—and they—stand on this issue. Do they desperately need to work from home because, for example, they have aging parents to take care of? Do you have a team job where they need to interact with a group most working hours? Your job as an interviewer is to find out if that match is going to work.

- Many interviewees want the job regardless of how well they match up with the criteria; and some companies prefer warm bodies, regardless of how well they match up with the criteria. But it is no secret that these types of arrangements generally do not work. Sometimes they work, but more often than not, the employee or the company suffers. Save yourself and the interviewee a lot of trouble—if the match ain't there, don't offer the job.

See <u>Tip 33: When and How to *Stop* an Interview</u> on how to bring an interview to an end before it is scheduled to finish.

- If it is going disastrously for you or the candidate, why drag out the pain?

See <u>Tip 36: Close It Down</u> on how to finish an interview well.

- There are specific steps to take to complete this process well. Suddenly picking up your papers, saying good-bye, and walking out is one way to do it, but not the most professional.

Real World Story

In one company I worked for, the guy I replaced had left before noon on his first day on the job. His stated reason: "This job was not what I expected it to be."

Perhaps that was true, but more importantly, that experience revealed the failure of both the interviewer and the candidate.

Whatever the candidate meant by his remark, it was clearly important enough to him that if the right question had been asked, he probably would have revealed his concern.

(We say "probably" because, as we detail throughout this book, things don't always go the way you expect them to. See <u>Tip 49: It Might Not Go Well Anyway</u>.)

- *Web Developer, 48*

Tip 15: Useful Interview Guidelines

Key Points

- The candidate may be nervous—some people cannot relax in an interview and that may not reflect their skill level.

- Some people are shy—very, very shy. A lot of geeks are shy.

- Don't talk the whole time! See <u>Tip 34: Common Hiring Mistakes</u> for more detail on this topic.

- Try to avoid simple questions with a "yes" or "no" answer.

- Always give the candidate time to ask his or her own questions.

Details

The candidate may be nervous—some people cannot relax in an interview setting and that nervousness may not reflect their skill level.

- Your job is to find the right candidate and to best do that, you need to determine if the person in front of you matches your criteria. Whether they can deal with the pressure of an interview may or may not be relevant to your criteria.

Some people are shy—very, very shy. A lot of geeks are shy.

- You may be hiring a sales engineer (where shyness can be a major liability), but you may be hiring a developer for your one-person office in Nome (where shyness might not even be noticed).

- To get around this issue, try asking questions that do not have a "yes" or "no" answer. Get them talking. (See <u>Tip 20: Ask Open-Ended Questions</u>.) Remember, they may be the best candidate for the job and the job may not require that they be articulate. Your main responsibility as an interviewer is to find the best candidate.

- A good question to ask them is: "If I called your boss today—with your permission, of course—what would they say about you?"

Don't talk the whole time! See <u>Tip 34: Common Hiring Mistakes</u> for more detail on this topic.

- You are interviewing *them*, not the other way around. Some talking on your part is required (we address what you should say in various tips, including <u>Tip 19: Basic Questions to Cover, Tip 21: Nontechnical Questions</u>, and <u>Tip 22: What Not to Ask</u>), but in general, you should be *listening*.

Try to avoid simple questions with a "yes" or "no" answer.

- If you make the interview more conversational, you will probably relax the candidate, but more importantly, you will probably get better answers from them, too. "Do you know Java?" is a simple and not very useful question. For one thing, you should already know the answer to that question from their resume. "What was your role in the last Java project you worked on?" is better; it gets them talking about their contributions and how they accomplished their goals.

Always give the candidate some time to ask their own questions.

- Good candidates should do several things: Research your company, research the role, and research you.

- This kind of information is readily available. Companies have websites; recruiters have job descriptions; professionals have LinkedIn profiles.

- All of that information is only part of the story, of course, and a good candidate will come prepared with his or her own list of questions to fill in the gaps. "Your website says you guys are moving into developing GIS software. Are you really doing that or is that just PR?"

- Other questions the candidate might ask have to do with topics or issues that came up during the interview.

- It is not a deal breaker if the candidate does not have questions, but it is a good sign if they do. Give the candidate time to ask them.

Notice how well they present themselves.

- Your job may require meeting clients; that can often mean a suit and tie, although that is no longer automatically true. But it does mean they must be *presentable*; someone can be presentable in shorts but someone else can be un-presentable in a three-piece suit. (For a real world story about this issue, see <u>Tip 39: Don't be Afraid to make 'Em Dance</u>.)

- You know what your company policy is; so determine if this person matches it and mark it down accordingly. If your company is looking for network installers or software developers, you may not need someone who owns a suit, but you still need someone who showers regularly.

Real World Story

Wow, presentation is everything—well, almost everything, anyway.

Focusing on technology is important, but when you have to have a conversation with a techie who doesn't find personal hygiene important, it is very uncomfortable.

I wish I would have focused on the "soft" side a bit more in some cases, and now I do it all the time. It was difficult to have the conversation to let someone—and a brilliant someone—know that they are awesome and the mission trip to Africa is very respectable, but they are back in the United States now and most people expect their co-workers to shower on a regular basis.

- *Team Lead, 25*

Tip 16: Let Management Know What You Need

In this economy—and *every* economy, actually—you should be able to explain in very clear terms why you need to hire for this position.

Key Points

- Make the justification as quantitative as you can.

- If possible, quantify the (potential) new hire's role.

- Some ideas on how to quantify the proposal include the following.

Details

Make the justification as quantitative as you can.

- This is easier said than done, of course, but it is also more important than it sounds. Many, *many* decisions in a corporation are made because of headcount, and you are asking to change that number.

- Examples of quantitative explanations include statements like: "Hiring another two programmers will increase our efficiency by 33%. That is only an estimate, of course, but past performance shows that increasing our headcount by 5% increases our productivity by a third."

- Keep the *Mythical Man-Month* theory in mind. ("…Adding manpower to a late software project makes it later.") Maybe quote it in your justification. But then explain why, like Moore's Law, the law is true in general but that specific applications may vary to a small degree.

If possible, quantify the (potential) new hire's role.

- "He or she will be handling the 150% increase in trouble tickets we have received since the recent merger."

- "Right now, we have three developers dealing with all six major sections of the application. Each section really should have its own developer since we have about the same level of functionality in each one. As a baby step toward achieving that goal, we should increase our technical staff by one."

Some ideas on how to quantify the proposal include the following:

- "The department's workload has grown by X% in the past year, and additional staff is needed to keep up."

- Sometimes you can justify the workload with metrics like the number of calls to the "Help Desk," the number of new projects, the company's growth, etc. Also, what about previous downsizing? (This is the "falling further behind" syndrome.)

- "The department has brought in new technologies and we need to hire people who are already skilled and experienced in order to use the product effectively."

- "The company can save time and money if certain processes are automated, but we need staff to implement and support this."

- "We will be able to respond to our users/customers X% faster if we expand our staff."

Real World Story

In my experience at several startup companies, even some late-stage startups, it has been extremely difficult to add more staff. Even when the work was overwhelming the current employees and management was spouting off about "growing the company," they usually meant more sales people and more employees to support the sales organization in marketing or other front-office positions. It's a funny reality—even in companies that develop software—that once the product reaches a certain stage, the focus is on sales and marketing and not developing new features.

While the frustration ate at me for a while, I finally learned how to communicate to upper management what was needed to grow the product to fulfill the needs of existing customers (while still keeping out an eye for new functionality and market opportunities). I had to become a salesman; but I wasn't selling a product, I was

selling the idea that the development staff had to
increase to grow the capabilities of the product.

Growing up writing software taught me to be
precise and detailed, but what I had to do now to
be successful was communicate and sell it at the
level of upper management. Sometimes it felt
dirty, but becoming proficient at PowerPoint was
necessary. Terseness was necessary; if it could
not be explained in one or two slides, my sales
pitch was lost. All that seems totally opposite of
the way it should be, but I realized it had become
a key requirement of the job.

- *Development Manager, 37*

Tip 17: How to Greet Interviewees

Remember your last interview? Even if you don't admit it, you were probably nervous. You might have been excited, interested, curious—but you were probably also nervous.

Now that you are on the other side of the table, spend a little time and effort trying to eliminate nervousness from the current hiring situation—make your candidate feel at ease.

Unless you are hiring for a high-pressure sales job (which is not the subject of this book), work to get the candidate relaxed—this will benefit both of you. A relaxed candidate will (generally) be more like the actual person and you can determine if you two can work together.

Key Points

- Be respectful of the candidate.
- Greet them promptly.
- Get over the initial jitters.

Details

Be respectful of the candidate.

- Keep in mind that respect is earned, not given. How you greet someone, especially a future employee, has the possibility to color the entire relationship.

- You only get one chance to make a first impression.

Greet them promptly.

- It's typical for a candidate to show up early, sometimes painfully early, to an interview. Some expect to be asked to fill out paperwork to apply once they are in the office. Others want to impress; "Hey, future boss, I'll be at work on time!"

- If you are in another meeting, have someone on the lookout for the candidate. If you can, excuse yourself from the meeting and go and greet the candidate, explain that you are in a meeting and give them a drink and someplace to be until the interview time. Then you can return to your meeting and begin the interview at the appointed time.

- If you can't leave the meeting, have that lookout perform the same function.

Get over the initial jitters.

- You know from your last interview that you were anxious, and your candidate will feel the same way. Repartees as you lead them to the area for the interview will go a long way towards calming someone.

- Small talk doesn't have to be about the company. "Hey, it's raining cats and dogs. I

hope traffic wasn't horrible getting here."
Put them at ease, and show that while you
are the boss, you're human too.

- You don't want the small talk to get out of
hand. If they start going on and on about
traffic, simply say, "Well, we need to get on
with the interview; let's get started."

Real World Story

I once met a candidate who was clearly flustered
when she came into the office—not the typically
anxiety, but far worse, nearly shaking. I put out my
hand for a handshake, explaining who I was and
confirming who she was, but I knew something
had happened.

I asked if she had any trouble finding the office, as
some of the nearby streets had similar names.
She informed me that she found it, but had a flat
tire on the way, a worst-case scenario for
someone going into a job interview.

I came back with some comment about how that
was horrible and I hoped the interview would be
memorable for reasons other than a flat tire, which
got a smile. Next was an offer for coffee or water,
and we were off to the interview.

The entire interview process was pretty well
scripted, including how to greet a candidate; and
since I had gone through training, I never really
registered what had happened. She was
eventually offered, and accepted, a job with the
company.

Years later, she told me more of her side of the story, and that how we first met for the interview really helped her calm down. She became a very valuable asset for the company, and she might not have gotten the job if she had been all wound up during the interview.

That simple exchange was valuable for her, and for the company too.

- *IT Manager, 40*

Tip 18: Prepare a List of Questions in Advance

No candidate is perfect. Some candidates are pretty damn close, though, so be ready. (And some are nowhere near even good enough, so be ready for that, too.)

Compile a list of criteria and rank them beforehand.

Then there is the well-known fact that every human on the planet sometimes forgets exactly what he or she is supposed to remember. Add to that the fact that interviews can be stressful for the interviewer, too, not just the interviewee, and you come to realize that by doing 15 minutes of thinking ahead can save you hours of extra effort.

You can do a more efficient job of hiring the person you need.

Key Points

- Compile a list of questions you need to know about every candidate.

- Sort that list before you go into the interview.

- Do they have soft skills?

- Can you imagine working *with* this person or even *for* this person?

- No interviewee in the history of mankind was perfect.
- Give the list of questions to the other interviewers.

Details

Compile a list of questions you need to know about every candidate *before* you go into the interview.

- You should be watching and listening to the candidate, not re-arranging your notes.

Sort that list.

- Rank the questions; you won't get to ask them all.

Do they have soft skills?

- How smart are they? How well do they seem to get along with others (see <u>Tip 23: Who Else Should Interview a Candidate?</u> on the value of team interviewing)? How self-motivated do they appear?
- They are called "soft skills" because they are hard to quantify, but that does not mean they don't manifest themselves in the real world.

Can you imagine working *with* this person or even *for* this person?

- We have all worked alongside people that are hard to work with for a variety of reasons; some types of individuals have a toxic effect on a workplace.

- Sometimes you can't tell in the interviewing process, but sometimes you can. Use the idea of them being a co-worker as a metric.

No interviewee in the history of mankind was perfect.

- Some were better suited for the job than others were, but no one is perfect.

- *One* of your jobs is to determine just how well suited Candidates A, B, C, and Z are for your position.

Give the list of questions to the other interviewers.

- Make sure that everybody has the list prior to the interview.

- If someone is pulled out of performing the interview, someone else should take their place.

- It will save everyone if everybody doesn't have to repeat every question during their part of the interview.

Real World Story

Once while being interviewed, I had the experience of a four-hour interview with what seemed like ten different people.

I've done enough interviews that I no longer care if it's a whole team interviewing me at the same time, or I get paraded through a bunch of offices and meeting rooms meeting a series of people.

But what gets my goat is when the interviewers are not prepared. Instead of really drilling down into technology subjects, every single interviewer comes armed only with a copy of my resume and asks me to tell them 'about my experience.' Clearly, they hadn't prepared for the interview or talked amongst themselves to discuss who was covering what subjects. As a job seeker knowing that I was going to talk to several people, I came in expecting some overlap. What I didn't expect was that everyone would do the same basic interview.

The only other conclusion I could make from the interview was that they were so swamped with work that they didn't have any time to get better at working. This conclusion sent up a red warning flag about working for the company.

In the end, I got a job offer from them but turned them down. Within three months, they were out of business. Whenever I think I'm crushed for time interviewing, I try to remember this experience and have vowed not to repeat it.

- *Web Developer, 35*

Tip 19: Basic Questions to Cover

Key Points

- How many years of experience using the technology in question do they have?

- Do they have a college degree?

- What kind of training/certification do they have?

- What specific hardware and software technologies are they familiar with?

- How many years of experience using the technology in question?

- Have two very specific questions you got from looking at their resume.

- Choose a few of these general questions.

Details

How many years of experience using the technology in question do they have?

- This is a very quantifiable topic and yet one that causes people to squirm. Ask this question casually; some large percentage of candidates will fudge their answer. (If candidate Andy claims "five years" of coding in a language, and you know that language has only been in use for four years, worry. Don't panic, but worry. A lot.)

Do they have a college degree?

- This is fast becoming a base requirement for many jobs. One reason is that they are easier to acquire online. But your position may or not require much breadth and it may never lead to any other position. Maybe you don't need this requirement. (See <u>Tip 26: Value of Education</u>.)

What kind of training/certification do they have?

- This type of criteria can be critical for some positions but completely irrelevant for others. Especially in these days of "one-day" certificates, weigh this need carefully. It is the kind of thing HR grabs onto tightly but which may cost you a better candidate. (See <u>Tip 24: The Value of Certification.)</u>

What specific hardware and software technologies are they familiar with?

- Be careful about being too specific with this requirement. Especially these days, asking for a person who can "code in the latest version of Ruby" may limit you too much. Or it might limit you *exactly* the way you want to be limited—you may need *only* people who can code in the latest version of Ruby.

How many years of work experience do they have?

- Regarding experience, there are lots of theories about what the right number of years for a particular job is. The multiple theories point to the old answer: "it depends." It depends on your work environment; if it is jammed with 20-somethings, you may want to think twice about bringing in someone with 25 years of work experience. It depends on your work requirements; if you need someone who can get up and running in your complex technical environment right away, you may not want someone right out of college.

Have two very specific questions you got from looking at their resume.

- "From your resume, I see that you worked at such-and-such company. Did you know So-and-So?"

- "I see from your resume that you have three years working with teams overseas. How did that go?"

- Don't make these questions too challenging; start slowly. You want to relax the candidate and relax yourself.

Choose a few of these general questions.

From the specific, consider circling back to the

general. Here are some generic questions you can ask to gauge the candidate's ability to think on their feet. You don't care about their specific replies; unless they are on the lam from federal agents at the moment, the details of their replies should not interest you. You care about *how they respond*.

- What do you know about our company?

- Tell me about your favorite job.

- Tell me what you liked least about your least favorite development job.

- If you were in this interviewer's chair, what would you ask?

- How do you feel about the rapid pace of change in our industry?

- How do you feel about risk?

- Have you finished *every* project on time? (Also say: "By the way, this is a trick question.")

- What work on this resume are you proudest of?

- Do you prefer working for large companies or small ones?

- How did you pick your college?

- Has the college major you chose worked out for you?

- How do you feel about travel?

Real World Story

One thing I've learned about the standard questions is that while you do *have* to ask these questions, they can actually produce good results. In addition to putting a check in the box that you asked the question, it also helps put the interviewee at ease. They expect these questions, which is good because you can get them out of the way fairly quickly while getting everybody in interview mode.

These questions also help me compare candidates because they are so standard. Open-ended questions can go anywhere. I jot observations down during opened-ended questions, but take even more detailed notes with the standard questions. More than once, reviewing the standard questions has helped me decide on a candidate when I have multiple contenders for a job opening.

• *Development Manager, 42*

Tip 20: Ask Open-Ended Questions

When the interview finally happens, you don't want to be caught unprepared and revert to questions like "Do you like Linux?" While that line of questioning may be useful time-killers, those kinds of questions will not uncover the hidden gems in your candidate. Remember, you're hiring geeks, folks who typically would get classified as INTJ (Introverted iNtuitive Thinking Judging). Interviewing these individuals is not the same as hiring a smiling receptionist; these folks can be arrogant and introverted at the same time. You need certain kinds of questions to pull out their best traits.

Key Points

- Problem solving, and software development in particular, isn't just about syntax.

- There are a lot of charlatans who could snow you in a brief interview.

- The skills and experience they have may not be exactly what you think you're looking for.

- Ask probing questions to uncover unexpected information.

- You have limited time to make the hiring decision.

- Listen for "I" statements.

Problem solving, and software development in particular, isn't just about syntax.

- A singular programming language, or several, may be important to your efforts. But do you really need another "expert" in one language, or someone who has skills that transcend one representation of a problem? Nothing in object-oriented techniques is tied to only C# or Java, the higher-level concepts of the components transfers. Your project and its design may be *impacted* by your platform of choice but it should not be *constrained* by the platform.

- UML exists to represent how software is constructed, and can be used to represent the sequence of events (among other concepts). Look back and analyze the last big failure of your product that took developers a longtime to correct. Was it a single line of code or did the developers' start throwing around words like "refactor"? That's an indication that you need design, not the syntax sugar of a single language.

There are a lot of charlatans who could snow you in a brief interview.

- Java, C++, C#, .NET, J2EE, XML, and the list keeps going. A candidate who scans your job posting can easily pick out what technologies and languages you are using. Google can fill in the rest of the information for a persistent searcher.

- Sure, you could give them a programming test, but what does this prove? Either you're going to find a simple test or you're going to dumb down a real problem you had to something they could solve in half an hour during an interview.

- It's great they had five years of C++ experience, but that was 10 years ago. How do you qualify that the candidate has stayed current with the recent changes and updates?

The skills and experience they have may not be exactly what you think you're looking for.

- Maybe you're hiring because your company is about to embark on a grand, new adventure. You may have a successful company and product, but now you need to deliver on a new platform. Maybe that platform is so new that you're not going to find the talent on the street. You need to look for a track record of conquering new technologies and applying them successfully.

- Sometimes you just can't ask for "five-plus years of experience" because the technology you need to use is a whopping six months old.

Ask probing questions to uncover unexpected information.

- Closed-ended questions can only be answered by specific responses and short answers.

- If you ask, "Up or down?" you can only get two possible answers. If you ask, "Have you used Java for five-plus years?" the candidate will either answer "Yes" or "No." You have learned nothing that you should have been able to glean from the resume. You did a good job wasting your time and the candidate's time.

- Open-ended questions yield the best results by expanding the possible answers and giving you insight into the candidate's experience.

You have limited time to make the hiring decision.

- You may only have half an hour to an hour with the candidate. You need to get the most out of that time for both of you.

- In your limited time, you need to find at least one reason hire this candidate over the others. If you only ask closed-ended questions, you have some numbers (Candidate A has five years as a DBA, Candidate B claims they have eight years, for example), but no real grasp of the whole problem. The longer experience could have come about in a position that mostly entailed contemplating their navel. If you only ask one style of question, you will never know the difference.

Listen for "I" statements.

- It's not universally welcome in the 21st century to brag about your accomplishments, as it is a reoccurring message throughout society to be a "team." It's unfortunate for some who want to pander to the lowest common denominator in people because, in an interview, you want to find stellar performers, not people who were only *on the same team* as stellar performers.

Real World Story

While interviewing for a software developer, the candidate was saying all the right words that matched the expectations of the job description. They had listed years of experience developing software with the languages that were in use at the company to which they were applying.

Then the open-ended questions began and something didn't feel right. On the surface, they were saying the right words in the right context, but when asked for deeper explanations, they floundered. Additionally, the answers were in the form, "We decided to …," "We built…," "We used…"

When finally asked point-blank what they did on the team, the answer was, "I wrote a build script."

It wasn't bad experience, but not what was
required for the job. If we hadn't asked open-
ended questions, we could have been snowed.

- *IT Director, 42*

Tip 21: Nontechnical Questions

Even the most technical positions require you to get some non-technical information from the candidate.

Key Points

- Here are some sample nontechnical topics you can raise and questions you can ask.

Details

Here are some sample nontechnical topics you can raise and questions you can ask:

- What do you think this job actually entails? Give me your description of it.

- What was involved in your last job?

- Tell me about your current manager.

- What is *not* on your resume that I should know about—professionally speaking only, of course? Are there jobs gaps, firings, etc.?

- Have you ever been laid off?

- Have you ever been fired for poor performance?

- Are you a 'geek' because you like it or because you can't do anything else?

- Tell me a hobby of yours.

- Tell me a little about yourself.

- What are your short- and long-term goals? Say "short term" means in the next six months, "long term" means three years.

- If you could change one thing about yourself professionally, what would it be?

- How do you define success? Failure?

- Do you consider yourself organized?

- Do you like change? Give me an example of how you embraced it (or, if you like, how you backed away from it).

- Why do you think I should hire you?

- How did you choose your college/your major? Was it a good decision?

- Who and why was your best manager and who was your worst manager (and why)?

- Why are you leaving your current company?

- What do you know about our company? (Assume they have been to your company website. If they haven't, that is a very bad sign. Every company—at least every company hiring computer geeks—has a website now. If an employee can't figure out that they should start their investigations into the new company there, they are probably not aware enough to bring much to your table.)

- Have you read, or heard, about any technology that you'd like to explore?

Real World Story

We frequently have to "sell" solutions internally within the company and sales expertise is not in a typical geek skill-set. The non-technical questions provide a window into how the candidate acts away from technology.

A good non-technical question is: "In five minutes or less, tell me why I should hire you?" That should get the blood pumping and bring out some personality quickly.

Before I learned this approach, I had made some serious hiring mistakes. By focusing only on technology, I totally missed all the touchy-feely stuff—the key inter-personal relationship topics that are so important to getting a large group working together well at a high level.

After having to deal with the downstream effects of not even peeking at the non-technical side of a person for several years, I now make it a priority to work in a couple of questions that stray from the straight up IQ and techy style of questions. As a side effect, my employee retention rate has improved.

- *Development Manager, 35*

Tip 22: What *Not* to Ask

There are questions in an interview that can cause *everyone*—candidate and interviewer alike—a lot of problems. Some questions can cause small problems, like frowns or evasions from the candidate, but others can cause large problems, like lawsuits. You don't want either.

Key Points

- Some very specific questions are illegal to ask a candidate in an interview. Do not ask about these issues.

- Here is a list of federally mandated topics to avoid.

- The liability for violating these laws is significant.

Details

Some very specific questions are illegal to ask a candidate in an interview.

- Do not ask about these issues. You should know this list backwards if you are involved in any stage of a hiring process.

Here is a list of federally mandated topics to avoid:

- Race (Civil Rights Act of 1964, Title VII)

- Color (Civil Rights Act of 1964, Title VII)

- Gender (Civil Rights Act of 1964, Title VII)

- Religion (Civil Rights Act of 1964, Title VII)

- National origin (Immigration Reform and Control Act of 1986)

- Birthplace (Immigration Reform and Control Act of 1986)

- Age (Age Discrimination in Employment Act of 1967, ADEA)

- Disability (Americans With Disabilities Act or 1990)

- Marital/family status, including children (Civil Rights Act of 1964, Title VII)

- Mental problems (Americans With Disabilities Act or 1990)

- Sexual Orientation (Civil Rights Act of 1964, Title VII)

- Arrest record (Rehabilitation Act of 1973)

The liability for violating these laws is significant. Don't play games with this.

- Many, many lawsuits arise from this issue. Stay away from these topics.

- Some people are tempted to finesse the topic by cleverly rewording questions, but the intent is the same. Don't do this! "Many, many lawsuits that arise from this issue."

Real World Story

As a young manager, I was in my very first round of hiring when I was presented with an interesting challenge during the hiring process. I had already done a phone screen, and the candidate sounded like an excellent one, with close to the skills and experience we were seeking.

When the candidate came in for the interview, I met him, made small talk to get him comfortable, and then we started addressing the technical issues.

I should have sensed something was different because he kept his hands folded neatly in his lap the entire time we were talking. Eventually I asked him to get up and draw out the problem on the white board. That's when I saw his hands; his fingernails were long and perfectly manicured.

He still appeared a little nervous, and I saw this as a chance to do a quick sidebar and hopefully put him at ease. I said, "Nice nails. Do you play classical guitar?"

While this is an innocent question on my part (I also play guitar and was honestly a little envious because nails like that would be natural fingerpicks!), the question backfired in a huge way.

He physically recoiled, like I had touched him with a live electrical cord. His answer was simply "No." But in that flash of recognition, we both knew something was up. But I ignored it and continued with the interview. In the end, he did have the skills to do the job and was hired. Later, we found out he was a cross-dresser, which made casual Fridays a little interesting.

Had I followed up with any more questions on the subject, my company and I could have been sued. I didn't know any better at the time. Now I know that any curiosity is tempered with a deeper understanding of what can and cannot be asked. Thankfully, it was innocent; and while we came right up to the edge of what was legal on that interview, neither of us crossed the line.

- *Software Development Manager, 25*

Tip 23: Who Else Should Interview a Candidate?

The more important a hiring decision is, the more important it is to have more than one person look at the same set of "facts." Sometimes, of course, having more than one person look at the data takes more time. And it is hard to do. (Think peer programming.)

But while it generally is not *easy*, it is a *good idea* to do it—much better end results are often the case.

Key Points

Typical questions about this issue include:

- Who else can help me interview candidates?

- Should you bring the team in at the very introductory stage?

- Should you have a semi-formal 'good cop/bad cop' routine?

- What if some people do not want to do this?

- How many people should a candidate interview with?

Who else can help me interview candidates?

- Potential "teammates" include your peers, your boss, employees from other departments, potential peers to the candidate, and someone from HR. It is *not* a case of 'the more the merrier,' but it *can* be the case of 'more than one set of eyes looking at the same data.'

- If you're hiring for a managerial role, it is common now to have people who will be managed by that person to participate in the interviewing process. (Remember, you are asking for their input, but *you* are making the final decision, not them.)

- There is a hidden benefit to this 'team' approach; everyone you ask to help you will feel more involved in building the company. (Also note that there will probably be a small minority of people *do not want* to feel more involved. This issue is addressed later in this Tip.)

Should you bring in the team at the very introductory stage?

- Actually, no; the most efficient approach is to narrow the candidates down to two or three, and *then* bring out your team of interviewers. Save the 'heavy artillery' for when it counts.

- The counter argument to the above is the idea that the candidate will have to face the fire at some point and it is better to have multiple opinions on a candidate before making a decision. But most companies wait until there are only a couple of candidates before doing multiple interviews. It costs too much to have all those man-hour cycles 'wasted.'

Should you have a semi-formal 'good cop/bad cop' routine?

- You don't need to go through that particular routine, but it is a good idea to have every interviewer responsible for asking several specific items. If you are hiring another developer for a section of code in one language, bring some of the other developers in that area into the interviewing process.

- Regardless of how formal you make it, you should have a brief pre-interview and post-interview meeting. It is more efficient *for everyone* if each person knows his or her role before the interview starts.

What if some people do not want to do this?

- Some companies make interviewing candidates part of every employee's responsibility and require formal pre- and post-interview meeting attendance.

- If you have an employee who balks at helping with interviewing, it can be helpful to point out to them that if they don't get involved at this stage, they have to live with the decision the rest of the team reaches without their input. A few well-placed examples of co-worker horror stories should do the trick.

How many people should a candidate interview with?

- There is no fixed number of required interviewers; some jobs really only need one interviewer, other positions need many more people involved.

- Not everyone must have *equal say* in the decision, however. Get their feedback but be clear that it is your decision (if that is true, of course), not theirs. You are asking for their *input*, not their decision.

Real World Story

What is the largest number of people you interviewed with for one job?

13 over three months and I *got* the job.

- *Scientist, 59*

12 over the course of four different meetings in three different states—and I did *not* get the job.

- *Account Rep, 24*

Tip 24: Value of Certification

Because they are so easily obtained, certificates don't have the value they used to have. Some certificates are still hard to get and very valuable—you're not going to get a CISSP by taking a weekend class online—but many are not.

Key Points

- Some jobs absolutely require a certification.

- Check out how valuable a particular certification is.

- It lets you know the candidate knows the basics but it does not let you know if they can think on their own.

- Can they solve problems on their own?

- Some certificates require persistence, which in and of itself is a good thing.

Details

Some jobs absolutely require a certification.

- A good example is "CISSP" (Certified Information Systems Security Professional). If you are hiring people for security work, this piece of paper matters.

- Others fall into the 'nice-to-have' category. A good example is "PMP" (Project

Management Professional.) If you need
someone to run a small project for a short
time, you probably don't need a certified
project manager. But if you have a project
with many personnel, millions of dollars,
multiple locations, etc., you would be much
better off hiring someone trained in that
level of complexity.

Check out how valuable a particular certification is.

- A quick search on the Web and a question
  or two for your colleagues or co-workers—
  or even asking the candidate themselves—
  can help you find out just how important this
  certificate is. Just because you have never
  heard of it may not mean it isn't valuable.

- When a certification (or college degree, for
  that matter), is in another country, it may be
  difficult to understand its importance. In
  these cases, you may have to find
  someone with the same cultural
  background to give you some perspective.
  For instance, very few US citizens would
  understand what a degree in Computer
  Science from the Indian Institutes of
  Technology (IIT) means to someone from
  India, unless they have had some
  experience working with outsourcing firms.
  The key point is: get help to understand the
  value before you make a judgment.

It lets you know the candidate knows the basics but it does not let you know if they can think on their own.

- Regurgitating test answers isn't what is needed on most jobs. Some certifications teach the basics, just the mechanics of a technology or approach, but don't teach you how to apply them in real world situations. Looking at it another way, do you want the musician that can play from rote memory, or the musician who can improvise on the fly in 7/8's time?

- Wiring up the same pattern of development again and again may be what you need in some situations (e.g. managing your Outlook email server should be done the standard way). But in others, you need that next level of creative spark to hook things together in new ways that will take your product or company to the next level of profitability.

Can they solve problems on their own?

- Sometimes you want to know if a candidate understands X or Y, but more often you want to know if they can think on their own.

- Can they solve problems—the types of problems your company solves—on their own?

- Say to yourself (not the candidate), "I know you have seen the *facts* required to solve the problem, but have you shown the *skills* to solve them?" Sometimes the same exact problem crops up, but often the same *kind* of problem crops up. Can the candidate recognize the problem and adjust?

Some certificates require persistence, which in and of itself is a good thing.

- Even if the 'piece of paper' is not particularly valuable, the fact that a candidate stuck with the program is a positive sign. Sometimes you can get a piece of paper by completing a few forms online, but sometimes it takes weeks or months of coursework to "pass." Maybe the content wasn't the most rigorous around, but the fact that the candidate made the time-commitment is a check in their favor.

Real World Story

I once helped place a woman who already had a more than 20-year career as an accountant. She was good at her job, but tired of doing the same thing and got the idea that something in IT would be a great second career. While she had used spreadsheets, even programmed macros, it wasn't enough to land a job doing something in software development.

We discussed her desire to take on the career shift, and the topic of certifications came up. She decided to go after a Microsoft SQL Server Certification.

After she finished the certification, she was easy to

place at an employer within a few weeks.

While she did take a short-term cut in pay, the longer-term benefit of being employed and constantly learning new technologies has paid great dividends. And in a few years, her salary exceeded her original salary. The employer received a mature individual with a work ethic and the persistence to go after new knowledge. It worked out great for her and her new employer.

- *IT Recruiter, 38*

Tip 25: Value of Commitment

Key Points

- Some people just coast through life.

- One way to test their commitment level is to evaluate the length of time the candidate has spent at a company.

- See if they stand for something away from the keyboard.

- Some people read the 'personal' section of resumes first.

Details

Some people just coast through life.

- That is fine, but you don't want those people on your team at work.

- You want people who are avid about things outside of work—so you can see that they have the enthusiasm for being avid workers. Their particular hobby does not matter—perhaps they play hockey or garden. Music and woodworking, by the way, in our experience, are often the hobbies of a certain kind of excellent coder. The parallels between programming, math, and music have been shown many times.

One way to test their commitment level is to evaluate the length of time the candidate has spent at a company.

- There are all kinds of reasons why an employee leaves a company, of course, but if the pattern is in frequently short stints (less than two-years; not as a contractor, but as a full time employee), be concerned.

- The opposite is also true. In this dynamic industry, if someone has worked for the same company for 15 years, be concerned.

- In both cases, ask the candidate about it directly. There may be perfectly legitimate reasons for either situation, but find out. (If they are surprised at the question, be very concerned. This is a well-known red flag.)

See if they stand for something away from the keyboard.

- Ask the candidate, read their resume, ask their references: Does this person stand for something? Everybody should (IMHO) be passionate about something. Even if you are hiring for a 'code monkey,' they should care strongly about something. It may not be coding—we are not advocating looking for a workaholic—but most people care deeply about something.

Some people read the 'personal' section of resumes first.

- Lots of people do not put anything personal on a resume, but lots more do. And some interviewers read this section first. They read this section because they are looking for commitment; they are looking to see if the candidate is interested in anything outside of work.

- Naturally, just because someone writes down "ice fishing" does not mean they are committed to it (although if they write, "ice fishing on the polar caps," you can probably assume they are into it a little bit).

Real World Story

Some people don't believe this, but geeks often *like to work.*

And they like to work on technical projects. They often work on 'technical projects' at home in their spare time.

They aren't casual woodworkers; they are often technically oriented woodworkers.

They aren't casual musicians; they are often technically oriented musicians.

Plenty of other types of workers like to work; geeks are hardly unique in this regard. We aren't saying this to praise or condemn them; we are simply stating a fact about what kind of people they are. They love working. If this quality does not shine in the interview, I ask about it directly.

"As you know, this is an intense position that will require a high degree of commitment. We are looking for someone who can put in a lot of time and energy toward meeting our goals. Have you made this kind of commitment before, and if so, how did you feel about doing it?"

- *IT Director, 45*

Tip 26: Value of Education

Key Points

- Some famous and rich guys in IT did not graduate from college.

- Not all college degrees and college majors are created the same.

- Use education as a weeding factor.

- How valuable—how *directly* valuable—is education to the job at hand.

- Should you care about famous schools?

- Do soft skills matter in an IT job?

- Are you asking for an advanced degree?

Details

Some famous and rich guys in IT did not graduate from college.

- Bill Gates, Larry Ellison and Mark Zuckerberg—guys who founded some of the world's largest companies and whose net worth's have nine zeroes in them—all never finished college. And yet, according to *US News and World Report*, 81% of the top 200 CEOs graduated from college.

Not all college degrees and college majors are created the same.

- Determine how important a college education is to *you* and how important a college education is to the *candidate*.

- Maybe a college degree is critical to you but trivial (because they don't have one) to a candidate. Maybe the opposite is true. Education may not necessarily be *the* factor, but it can be *a* factor.

Use education as a weeding factor.

- There are many statistics—we are not going to quote them here, but you can easily find them on the Web—about the success rate of people who graduate from college.

- In Boom times (for you, the hiring manager), you need all the legitimate weeding tools you can get. (Gender is *not* a legitimate weeding tool BTW. Just saying.) Use a college degree as a criterion when you hand your list over to HR.

- In Bust times (for you as a hiring manager), read the next section about determining the direct and indirect value of an education to the position you are hiring for.

"How valuable—how *directly* valuable—is education to the job at hand?" is perhaps the wrong question.

- IT changes so fast that very few colleges offer courses with direct, immediate value to technical positions. That is an exaggeration, of course, but it is not without merit. Even the most technically-oriented community colleges have a hard time staying abreast of the sea changes that sweep through the industry all the time.

- Given that the pace of change is ferocious, you should aim not for what is right in front of you, but what is six months to a year out.

- The position you are hiring for may not require anything remotely like a business degree, but will this person eventually become a manager that needs to talk to the business side of the company?

- The position you are hiring for may not require anything remotely like a hard science degree, but will this person eventually become a manager that needs to talk to the research side of the company?

Should you care about famous schools?

- Estimates are that there are over 4,000 colleges and universities in the United States alone. You have not heard of most of them.

- Estimates are that there are over 600 college majors. You have not heard of most of them.

- Don't assume. Degrees from prestigious universities can mean a lot—or they can be trivial. The point is not to assume that just because someone has a degree from some famous technology institute in Massachusetts, for example, they are perfect for your position. That degree gives them a lot of cred technically, but there are plenty of other things you need to find out about the candidate before you offer them the job.

- Don't assume they are great—or are terrible—candidates because they attended a famous school. Do your homework during the interview. Ask specific questions about the course of study, for example, or try to extract concrete information about the candidate's time there. Was there a lot of work done, or a lot of alcohol consumed?

Do soft skills matter in an IT job?

- Yes. They are not the only thing that matters, of course, but they are critical.

- If the person has a degree in one of the social sciences (e.g., psychology), they may have greater skills in user-oriented activities (support, training, process improvement, designing interfaces, etc.). They may have a greater ability to see things from a different perspective and not be limited by the idea of "there is only one right answer." Start with this assumption and verify it with further questioning.

Are you asking for an advanced degree?

- In Bust times (for candidates, when jobs are hard to find), many people acquire additional degrees.

- Advanced degree holders generally want more money for their extra coursework. Sometimes this request is valid; sometimes it is not. Be aware of this tendency.

Real World Story

I attended a prestigious university, but I never reveal the name on my resume. The school was famous for other things besides its technical prowess, and I did not want to spend even a fraction of my interview time talking about accomplishments I had nothing to do with.

I got a job with a company downtown and it went very well. Six months after I got the position, the hiring manager overheard me telling an admin at a company cocktail party where I went to school.

He was shocked, and came over and told me he had no idea that I went to that college.

I replied that I never reveal that fact in interviews. He then revealed that if he *had* known, he *never would have hired me*. Apparently, he had hated "my school" since he was young.

- *Web developer, 48*

Tip 27: Take Notes *During* the Interview

After you interview five candidates, they start to blur. They might all be very similar, but more likely a couple of them are terrible and a couple of them are just OK.

Write something down *every* time.

Key Points

- Sometimes you don't have time to prepare a list of questions before you interview.

- Do a little thinking in advance or you might miss some very important facts.

- Some people are brilliant interviewers.

- After you interview five candidates, they start to blur.

- Be careful how you take notes.

- Regardless, you should always scribble a few notes after every interview.

Details

Sometimes you don't have time to prepare a list of questions before you interview.

- Make notes on the resume *before* you walk in. Make notes on the resume *while the candidate is talking.*

Do a little work in advance or you might miss some very important facts.

- If the interview ends and you have not discovered the three key facts about the person—they spent the last four years in prison, for example, or learned programming last year from an online class, or want a job where they can work from home anytime they want—you have failed as an interviewer. These facts might or might not be deal breakers for your company, but you should have known about them *before* the person was hired.

- You might get a bonus for employing someone into the hire-a-former-prisoner program or you may get chewed out for hiring someone who never shows up for the Friday staff meetings. Find out that stuff beforehand.

Some people are brilliant interviewers.

- Whether it's because of their previous training or because that is what they do all day, some people do a great job of interviewing other people. If you watch these folks, they arrive to interviews with notes or they take notes during the interview. (The interviewee is occasionally both flattered and flustered.) :-)

After you interview five candidates, they start to blur.

- They might be all very similar, but more likely a couple of them are terrible and a couple of them are great. Write that down.

Be careful how you take notes.

- Some people (not many anymore!) can read handwriting upside down, so you should either write notes in your code or jot things down so that the candidate cannot see it.

Regardless, you should *always* scribble a few notes after *every* interview.

- Even if it is only "Jack: red polo shirt, rude; clueless about new version of Java." Or "Mark: business suit; knows Ted G. and learned Flex at last job."
- Write something down every time.

Real World Story

I have been on multiple interviews where one person's only job is clearly to take notes. They do not say anything unless they are spoken to. This can be somewhat unnerving for the candidate, but it clearly relaxes the interviewers. They feel free to focus on the interview and let someone else take notes.

But in two situations at least, right before the interview was scheduled to end (and *after* I had a chance to ask my questions), the lead interviewer turned to the note-taker and asked, "Is there anything we missed?" They had been taking notes, but they had also been tasked with making sure the key questions were asked.

* *Developer, 45*

Tip 28: Offering the Correct Amount for an IT Position

If you're currently hiring, and have been for a while, then you already know the market value for the skills you're seeking.

If you haven't hired for a while, it may be difficult to kick-start the process of hiring. A big hurdle is knowing what you *should* pay (given the current market for the skills) and what you're *able* to pay (given your company's constraints).

Key Points

- Your hiring budget gives you a place to start.

- Recruiters are a great source of information.

- Your current employees can be a valuable supply of contacts.

- The candidates themselves, amazingly, can often be good resources.

Details

Your hiring budget gives you a place to start.

- You may find yourself with a pre-determined amount from your company; the budget was set, and you're basically stuck. If the budget isn't sufficient to enlist the level of talent you need, keep reading and be prepared to sell the notion that you need more in the budget to fill the position.

- If you don't have a set budget, you need to determine what the going rate is in your area for the skill set you need.

Recruiters are a great source of information.

- You're the hiring manager, and you get the phone calls and emails from recruiters wanting to "be of service" all the time. Well, it is time to take them up on that offer and ask a question: "What's the rate for X?" If it's a common skill, they will know off the top of their heads. (If they don't, move right along to the next recruiter).

- Many recruiters publish salary surveys. Save these, but keep only the current publications. These are useful for two reasons. First, you have a handle on what the current market will pay for various skill sets. Second, you should check that your current employees are not dramatically under-market—especially the employees you want to keep. Chances are they have received the same information. (See <u>Tip 10: The Good, Bad, and Ugly about Using Recruiters</u>).

Your current employees can be a valuable supply of contacts.

- Chances are that your employees know others who also work in the IT industry. For new positions, with a skill set that you don't currently have on your staff, your existing employees are a great source of information. Simply asking the existing staff if they know of anyone working with a technology often gets results.

The candidates themselves, amazingly, can often be good resources.

- Sometimes you have no knowledge or insight into what money a particular skill set brings in the marketplace. Post the job anyway with a good description. You can ask in the first couple of phone screens what the candidate is currently making, and then use that information to help put a price on what you will need to pay.

Real World Story

In the mid-1990s, in the halcyon days before the dot-com bust, the market for IT skills was changing dramatically. Skill with technologies that were not commonly on anyone's radar a few years before were now suddenly "must-haves" for every employer. It's frightening that the teens of the 21st century think of frames in HTML as once being cool, but they were, and it was all new to people in the IT industry then.

Suddenly, or at least it felt sudden to me at the time, I found myself in a position of hiring for jobs that required skills, TLAs, and technologies that I had no background in myself, nor did anyone on my staff. We had to turn the ship quickly to move our product from a PC-based delivery to the new world of a thin client browser, in web pages and a bunch of stuff that a few months before were unheard of. We didn't know what to pay, and had a set budget with little room for wiggle. The data from recruiters sending salary surveys was mashed up (not a term we had at the time!) with information we sought at a conference. We had to come up with a budget and determine how many people we could hire to jump-start our product development with new technologies.

At this point, the only info we had was what recruiters were feeding us and by looking at job postings in the newspaper and the fledgling sites that were online at the time. The realization was that you must pay what the market will bear for a skill set when you are in desperate need.

I never forgot the lesson this experience taught me, and now keep an eye on the job postings in my city for the skills I know I will hire for and new skills that I might need someday soon.

- *Software Development Manager, 30*

Tip 29: Other Ideas Besides More Money

At some point it's all about the top line; we say *top* line because that is how much money people "think" they make. They can brag that they make $125,000, but what's the big deal?

Sure, you can choose to reduce the effective number with 401(k) contributions or a health care flexible spending account, and maybe it's required that you purchase a parking pass; and then nothing is as certain as taxes, except death. In the end, very, very few geeks are bringing home a bottom line of $125,000. Companies don't pay that kind of money for most technical talent.

So how else can you compensate a geek besides cash?

Key Points

- Sometimes geeks want other things besides money.

- Time off is important, too.

- Non-standard benefits can be very valuable to some people.

- Variable compensation is another valuable idea some employees love.

Details

Sometimes geeks want other things besides money.

- Let's face it; the next job is as important as the current job. Sure, people appreciate loyalty; longevity at one employer can mean becoming fully vested in a 401(k). But techies also want to get their hands on the latest and greatest technology. It may pad their resume for that next job, and the employer reaps the benefits as well as realizing improvements in the existing products.

- State-of-the-art tools, in both the hardware and software side of technologies, help keep the interest of geeks. It also pays dividends in unexpected places; having an 8-core desktop machine for software developers will get them threading software to take advantage of that horsepower and by doing so give you an upgrade path in your production environments.

- Being on the "Tiger Team," working on the next hot product, is always exciting and feeds the geek's ego. At the same time, don't disrespect those working on your legacy products, because that is what brings home the bacon *today*.

Time off is important, too.

- Quit splitting "vacation" and "sick" time; merge it into "PTO" (Paid Time Off). Quit making people lie about being "sick" to take a day off. PTO should be flexible enough that an employee can take two hours for a doctor appointment without jumping through flaming HR hoops.

- Developers are famous for making long runs at the computer. The tradeoff is that doing that every day is a path to burnout, which is a problem not only for the employee but also for the employer as the employer ends up getting less quality work. Think about the time the developers put in and how they work. Why not go with a 9x80 schedule where every other Friday is a day off? That gives time for work, and time to hit the beach or go snowboarding without cannibalizing work time.

Non-standard benefits can be very valuable to some people.

- Is your office near the public transit line? Think about an employer-paid pass to sweeten the pot. Not only will the employee have a method to get to work, they can use it for personal trips.

- Do you develop for mobile applications? Get them the latest-and-greatest phone and operating system combination and pick up the bill.

- What is your dress code? Is casual Friday with jeans enough? If you're not in a customer-visible portion of the business, what's wrong with everyday being casual? In the summer, make a rule that shorts are an option between Memorial and Labor days. (Just no "Daisy Dukes!")

- A work-from-home day is sometimes welcome. Letting this become a free-for-all is a bad route, as you cannot gauge what work is getting done. If you do implement any work from home, make sure you have clear goals regarding your expectations of tasks completed before you allow work from home.

Variable compensation is another valuable idea some employees love.

- If you are developing software with agile methodologies, why not attach a bonus on hitting all the goals for each iteration?

- How about a small bonus for code quality? Be sure you can measure quality before you can implement this bonus.

Real World Story

One reason I stayed at an employer for as long as I did was the fact that they had a 9x80 schedule. Every other Friday was a day off, with the caveat that you put in your 80 hours on the other nine working days. It worked fantastically, as it allowed for putting in long stretches programming and an extra day off to head up to the mountains for skiing before the traffic became horrible.

One issue in advance had to be managed because it threw a wrench into the machine. At first, everybody wanted Friday off, but there are only two Fridays in every two weeks. The problem was solved by a lottery held by pulling names from a hat twice a year.

The unexpected benefit was that it gave QA a day without (or at least fewer) changes to the code because inevitably the developers wanted Fridays to hit the slopes. Then QA took Mondays off at their 9x80, giving them a three-day weekend, while the developers could concentrate on fixing what QA had found on Friday without new issues being reported right in the middle of development.

- *Java Developer, 35*

Tip 30: Have a "D-IQ"
(Developer IQ)

- You have to cover a lot of ground in a short amount of time.

- A little knowledge about a lot of things is good.

- Keep it quick and have fun.

- Ask how they feel about a particular technology.

- Questions for someone who needed at least a passing familiarity with RDBMS and SQL include the following.

Details

You may have to cover a lot of ground in a short amount of time.

- The time you—and your candidate—have allotted for this interview is important. This can be a complex issue to address quickly.

- There are a lot of technologies that you need a resource to be familiar with, but not necessarily an expert. As long as the GUI people have a passing familiarity with SQL, for example, you may be good to go; the middle-tier developer might have to have intimate knowledge of SQL, execution plans, etc. to make the team work.

- While individual technologies may be outside of the scope of the position today, you can't anticipate exactly what you'll need in the future. If the candidates are at least aware of advances outside of their core responsibilities of their job, they have an interest in technology and that may be very valuable in the future.

A little knowledge about a lot of things is good.

- Since you can't predict everything you'll need to use in the future, or even what your customers may ask for next year, the fact that the candidate has some idea about technologies you are not currently using can be beneficial.

- Looking at a problem in a different way can lead to better solutions. The push and pull of technology continues to drive innovations. For decades, SQL has been dominant and yet there are emerging technologies for NOSQL databases that look at the storage and retrieval problem in a different way.

- A spark of inspiration may be just what it takes to drive your product to another level. If you are only interested in the technologies you are using today, you could be missing out on some wonderful ideas.

Keep it quick and have fun.

- The purpose of the Developer-IQ portion of an interview is to cover a lot of ground quickly. The Developer-IQ should cover a wide variety of topics.

Ask how they feel about a particular technology.

- To avoid yes/no answers, ask the candidate for their feelings about a technology. If they have experience with something that was necessary to include but sucked to use, you're not going to get a complimentary response. On the other hand, if they have used it in the past and it was perfect for their application, they may be jumping out of their seat to tell you more.

- It covers a lot of topics fast and discovers the breadth of knowledge of a candidate quickly.

Questions for someone who needed at least a passing familiarity with RDBMS and SQL include:

- When does a trigger fire?
- What is a star schema?
- What's a snowflake schema?
- What is an outer join?

These quick questions drilled a candidate on database knowledge much further than "How long have you used SQL? The questions got behind the scenes of a database, and dug deeper faster than asking the candidate about the select or where clause of an SQL statement, while also getting into topics like outer joins and how they are different.

Real World Story

One time we were hiring a completely new team and we had to staff up quickly.

While we knew what legacy technologies we needed to use, we also knew that it would be rapid development and that we didn't know what technologies we would need in the future.

We needed to do a lot of interviews in a short time and be able to end the interview if we knew there was no match for the candidate or the company. To cover the basics very quickly, we asked a list of short questions that could not be answered with just one word but needed to be answered with a sentence or two.

The next section was where we asked for *feelings*—probably the only time in the interview where subjective responses were acceptable! It could cover a lot of topics lighting fast and discover the breadth of knowledge of a candidate very quickly.

If we were interviewing for a Java developer, the lightning round to get gut reactions would contain topics like:

- .net

- J2EE

- SOA

- ESB (two proper answers here, both equally accepted: Enterprise Service Buss or Extra Special Bitter.)

- Eclipse

- SourceForge

If they didn't know what SourceForge was, then how would they know where to go find a pre-existing html parser or 100's of other software components? While it's a fun academic project to write everything yourself, most companies are not going to afford the time to have a developer write, test and debug an XML parser when a perfectly good one (example: jDom) could be downloaded in less than a minute.

- Slashdot

After asking about "Slashdot," the candidate might reply, "It used to be a great source for coding stuff but lately a lot of politics." That's a fine answer; it shows that they know what Slashdot is, how to find it, and what to you can get from Slashdot.

- *Software Development Manager, 40*

Tip 31: Things to Watch Out For

Key Points

- There are many people who over-promise and under-deliver.

- Are the facts on their resume correct?

- Have they ever completed anything in their lives?

- A classic hiring landmine statement is, "I never knew I had to…"

- Personal hygiene issues are tricky but they can be critical, too.

Details

There are many people who over-promise and under-deliver.

- These people are not always easy to spot; sometimes they make things easy by claiming to have invented Java or something, but more often, their fakery is more difficult to spot. During the interview, do your best to determine that they have ownership of the knowledge they claim to own. Open-ended questions are a great way to really dig into what they know.

Are the facts on their resume correct? (See Tip 11: How to Read a Resume.)

- Do they really have three patents to their name, or were they working in a company that got three patents while they were there?

- When discussing other compensation options (see Tip 29: Other Ideas besides More Money), do they pounce at the idea of working from home? This may be a benefit in your company or it may be a deal-breaker; regardless, it is good to know this in advance.

Have they ever completed anything in their lives?

- Software development is ever ongoing; infrastructure network construction is ever ongoing; trouble-ticket solving is ever ongoing. But that does not mean that the people working on these projects do not complete tasks. Some projects have distinct start and end dates. Many tasks that are part of these projects have distinct start and end dates.

- And some people cannot meet deadlines. Some can, but many cannot. This is not easy to determine in an interview, but you should try. Ask questions like: "Tell me about a project or large task that you successfully completed." Or, "I am always interested in candidates' project management skills. Can you give me a brief example of a project you started, worked through, and finished?"

- If they say it was "cool," "easy," or even if they say, "It was brilliant!" then you should be worried. Ask more probing questions like "If you had to go back and start that project over today, what new technologies would you use?" and "What was a difficult bug after the release and how did you correct it?" Don't accept their simple and exciting description as the final word on the topic.

A classic hiring landmine statement is: "I never knew I had to..."

- It might save you and the candidate a lot of time and effort if you spend a little time—even in the initial interviews—talking about some of the specifics of the job. Often, you are not really looking for a candidate who can do Task X and Task Y. Few jobs are so clear-cut. What you are looking for is a candidate who can do Task X and Task Y *and* Task Z—the task that suddenly appears in mid-job. Then, *on their own*, figure out that Task A and Task B are also required.

- If a candidate is only looking to do his or her exact responsibilities, it is best if you know that up front. You may be fine with that—some jobs, such as many data entry jobs, are like that—but most jobs require some flexibility. Naturally, there are limits— if you neglect to mention that all employees must travel over 75%, you are setting yourself up for problems when people join your team. But more often, the candidate will respond with "I never knew I had to…" Try and cut this problem off at the source.

Personal hygiene issues are tricky but they can be critical, too.

- While tricky from an HR perspective, this issue is a landmine for you and your team. One question several managers have faced is: "Is showering a personal hygiene option?" or, put another way, "Is *not* showering a personal hygiene option or does it affect more than just one person?" It may sound obvious to members of certain cultures where perfume is a necessity, but members of other cultures feel differently.

- If you are operating a cube farm or other working environment with multiple people working next to each other all day, how people feel about personal hygiene matters.

- You (and the candidate) should consider the interview persona they present as 'the best they can do.' If they are not 'looking good' for that event, move quickly on to the next candidate. (See <u>Tip 33: When and How to *Stop* an Interview</u>.)

Advance degree holders want more $$ for their extra coursework.

- You may or may not want to pay extra for the additional education the candidate flashes before you. Sometimes you can simply ignore the extra degree; but many (not all, but many) advance degree holders are not going to let the issue go by unnoticed.

- The best approach is to prepare your job description carefully; and in your preparation, determine if advance degrees are required, a hindrance, or irrelevant to the position.

- If you do this before you walk into the interview, you'll be ready when the candidate inevitably brings it up. You might grimace, you might grin with delight, you might ignore the topic, but in any case, you'll be ready.

Real World Story

Perhaps the most amazing interview story I have heard was one from a colleague.

We interviewed a guy right out of college for an entry-level sales job. After several people spoke to him, he seemed fine and we offered him a position.

Monday morning of the following week rolled around and he was supposed to report to work. After two hours, I called his house.

- "Oh, I am not working for your company."

- "Well, it was certainly nice of you to tell us. Why not?"

- "Because you are on the second floor."

- "What?! Why not?!"

- "I can't work for a company that is on the second floor. I am scared of heights."

This story *really did* happen. If you doubt it, you have not been hiring people very long.

- *Senior Project Manager, 45*

Tip 32: Watch Out for the New Guy Who Can't Code

Key Points

- You need to hire smart people who get things done.

- Don't hire inept people.

- New hires can frustrate you.

Details

You need to hire smart people who get things done.

- These two concepts go hand in hand. Academia is ripe with smart people, but what have they accomplished? Written a textbook or taught a class? Those are valuable things, but don't directly translate to the day-to-day work of producing a piece of software that users find valuable and are willing to pay $$ for with their hard earned money.

- When it costs so little to register a domain name, or get registered as a developer for Android, why doesn't every developer not have a website or mobile product of their own? If they don't, you need to be ready for a lot of talk in your office about current TV shows, because that's what they are doing in their spare time—sitting on their butt watching TV. You want the developer who you are in constant danger of losing because some crazy idea they had paid off. That's the talent who can take your product to the next level.

Don't hire inept people.

- Asking questions like "Why are manhole covers round?" or starting the interview with the classic FizzBang (a.k.a. FizzBuzz) problem are great ways to quickly weed out a candidate. Once done with the weed-out portion (which should happen in a phone screen or at least long before you bring in five people to interview the candidate), move on to what they have accomplished.

- Inept people won't have contributed much to their last employer. While spending time in meetings planning is necessary, if they *only* planned and didn't create anything, do you really want them on your team?

New hires can frustrate you.

- If you've been managing software developers for any length of time, you've been told that it takes six months to get up speed on the product by at least one of your developers. That's a cop-out, because there is a high probability you have a task that would take at most a couple of days and would teach the new hire all of your processes and procedures along the way. Getting a new hire contributing and successful right away leads to your success as a manager of these skilled workers.

- Letting a newbie sit and work on a large task is a bad approach. They will struggle, asking very basic questions that should be red flags of their ignorance. When a work product finally does emerge, it will be riddled with bugs, maybe even so bad that you'll be forced to "refactor" it completely and start over.

Real World Story

The company I was working for was hiring at a very rapid pace. There was a new person starting every day, and still the work that needed to be accomplished was overwhelming. Unfortunately, due to the rapid pace of development, it was also easy for a few people to coast because there was so much going on in the development that it was difficult to track each individual.

When I finally could concentrate on the contributions of individuals, there was one sticking out like a sore thumb. Everything this person checked in was a constant source of bug reports from QA, and contained even more surprises when we got to production. He was an avid reader of blogs and books on software development, and from that reading, knew all the right words. Problem was, he knew the words but had never applied any of the concepts successfully. The code was full of great names like "Factory," "Inheritance," "Interface," "Abstract Class," "Information Hiding," and "The Open/Close Principal." At first glance, it looked like a textbook of good programming practices. But inspecting the code revealed a different picture: none of it was "Object-Oriented," methods were huge (200+ lines of code) and there was no understanding of memory management in a highly available system and so on. The code contained all the right words, but the implementation was far from professional.

It took nearly a year for these problems to surface, but when it finally had a light shone on it, the code crumbled. Faced with the insurmountable task of correcting the bugs and maintaining the code in the future, the person quit.

At least the decision to keep them or fire them was made for me, but ultimately the responsibility landed in the lap of management. In retrospect, the interview should have sent up warning signs because this person had never been at a job longer than six months, even though they had been in the industry for years. They had no projects of their own. It was a disaster that I vowed never to repeat.

- *Software Development Manager, 41*

Tip 33: When and How to *Stop* an Interview

Key Points

- Your time is valuable.

- Like meetings, job interviews can go *less* than their allotted time.

- Sometimes, go the allotted length.

- Sometimes, cut it off quickly.

- Sometimes, let it go over.

- What is the right length of time for an interview? The answer, obviously, is "It depends."

Details

Your time is valuable.

- You have a job and maybe interviewing candidates is part of it, or maybe it isn't.

- Regardless, you don't have time to waste.

Like meetings, job interviews can go *less* than their allotted time.

- It is not only *legal* to do so, but it is often in *everyone's best interests* to do so.

- As the person driving the interview process, it is up to you to determine when the right time to end an interview.

Sometimes, go the allotted length.

- If it is scheduled for an hour and it seems to be going well—progress is being made—let it go for the entire time. This is the default behavior.

Sometimes, cut it off quickly.

- If it is scheduled for an hour and both you and/or the candidate quickly discover that this relationship is not going to work, don't prolong everyone's pain.

- Don't waste your time or theirs—end it. It really is more respectful to end the interview than drag it out just because your Blackberry says you don't have another meeting for 45 minutes.

Sometimes, let it go over.

- If it is scheduled for an hour but the position is important enough—and your uncertainty about the candidate merits the extra time— let it go over.

- Sometimes things look very promising, but the initial allotted time turns out not to be enough. Either the conversation took unexpected (but positive) directions or something else happened. Extend the initial interview if you can.

What is the right length of time for an interview? The answer (obviously) is "It depends."

- The overall point is: the right length of time for an interview depends greatly on how it progresses. Some interviews should be cut off quickly, others should be allowed to spill over.

- Be ready for various possibilities and don't assume that because it is scheduled for a certain time that you have to use that time. Use less or more as needed.

- Remember the adage that "work expands to fill the available time." If you schedule two hours, it will take two hours.

- But think back on your own experiences; how much of those two-hour interviews you had were just "filler" as opposed to real content?

- If you can get the interview done in half an hour, make it half an hour.

Real World Story

I have cut interviews off where I was the interviewee. Why waste everyone's time?

In one case, the interviewer started the conversation with a statement about how important advanced degrees from prestigious universities mattered at his company. It was clear to me that my school was not prestigious enough for him.

A few more 'pleasantries' and I told him his 'political interview' (he had clearly needed to go through the motions of talking to someone outside the company before hiring the internal candidate) was over and I walked out.

* *Web Developer, 40*

Tip 34: Common Hiring Mistakes

Key Points

- Don't define the position poorly.

- Don't hire for political reasons, instead of valid team and required skill ones.

- Don't talk the whole time.

- Don't neglect the background checking stuff.

- Be careful you're not hiring just clones of yourself.

Details

Don't define the position poorly.

- See <u>Tip 7: Write Down a Job Description</u> for a discussion about how to define a position well. Both candidates and the company should have a very good idea of what the position requires. Your needs will probably change, of course, but they are probably not going to change that much. If you are hiring a DBA, the skills to do that job are pretty well defined. If you are hiring an internal phone support person, the skills for that position are pretty well defined. If you are hiring a "utility player," you have a bigger challenge ahead of you.

- Neither you nor your co-interviewers really know what you are looking for. Remember, as we discuss in <u>Tip 18: Prepare a List of Questions in Advance</u>, this is not a good time to be winging it. Be ready.

Don't hire for political reasons instead of valid team and required skill ones.

- Sometimes you *have* to hire the boss's son, in which case you might be able to mitigate the problem by making him an intern first or having him report to your least-favorite manager.

- But if you have a choice in the matter, be very, very careful about making political hires. Earlier (see <u>Tip 14: Conduct the Best Type of Interview</u>) we discussed the fact that there are no perfect candidates, often only several 'good enough' candidates. And in that situation, if the political hire ("The new manager attended temple with one of the VPs in a company I worked for.") is just as viable as the other candidates, go for it.

- But that is often *not* the case; the political candidate is often not as qualified as some of your other choices. The best way to prevent this problem is to head it off at the pass; promise a political *interview*, but be clear that does not mean a political *hire*. It can be tricky, we know, but the short-term pains can be far outweighed by long-term gains.

Don't talk the whole time.

- It is a common mistake for the interviewer to talk a great deal during an interview. They can do this for several reasons, including the fact that the interviewer may be nervous, he likes to talk about his own job, he is not prepared, etc. Regardless of the reasons, don't do it! The simple fact of communication is: if you are talking, you are not listening. And if you are not listening, you aren't finding out anything about the person in front of you.

Don't neglect the background checking stuff.

- As we discuss in <u>Tip 3: How to Get Help with Your Hiring</u>, you don't have to do this yourself. If you have an HR department, use them. In many organizations, they will insist on doing this themselves. (There is a right and wrong way to do them.)

- But don't neglect to do it. Some companies go to great lengths: they require drug tests or credit checks in addition to a specific number of reference checks. If your company does not require background checks, you should do a minimum anyway and at least contact several of the references listed. Keep in mind that the candidate has probably prepared these people in advance (although not always!) and that some people feel very constrained in how they can respond. But do it anyway.

- It is becoming standard to run a simple Google search and looking on social media sites like Facebook before a candidate is hired. The legality of this is still fluid, but any geek who is not aware of how they appear on the Web might be a little too narrow-minded for you.

Be careful you're not just hiring clones of yourself.

- You may really like your working style, but keep in mind that in many areas of life, including the workplace, etc., there are often multiple ways to solve a problem. And many of those ways are equally valid. Keep that in mind when you hear candidates talk about themselves and their work; it may not have been how you would have done it, but it might be a perfectly legitimate approach.

Real World Story

I have received *two* job offers from two different companies where I said almost nothing and the interviewer talked the entire time; at the end of the interview both interviewers said: "You sound like a great candidate—when can you start?"

I was flabbergasted. I had been offered the job - the interviewer knew little about me. They had seen my resume, of course, but as we discuss in <u>Tip 11: How to Read a Resume</u>, a resume is only a part of the package. It is only a percentage—and sometimes not a significant percentage—of what the person can bring to the table.

- *Junior Technical Writer, 31*

Tip 35: It Might Not Go Well Anyway

Key Points

- Things seldom go according plan.
- *Your* circumstances could change.
- *Their* circumstances could change.

Details

Things seldom go according plan.

- Interviewing and hiring are no different from writing code or installing a new server—you are better off accepting that there are going to be some deviations and be prepared for them instead of crying all the way home.

Your circumstances could change.

- Your company could suddenly implement a hiring freeze in the middle of your interviewing process. You could get promoted and suddenly not need to worry about filling this particular position; there all kinds of valid reasons why the interview process may radically change directions for you.

Their circumstances could change.

- You may like them but they may not like you; you make them an offer but discover that they have changed their minds about looking for work because they have decided to move to another city or go back to school. Don't faint. Go on to your next candidate.

- Remember that they are probably interviewing at other companies. But be careful about hearing that there is another job offer on the table. It may be tempting to counter-offer and increase the compensation, but unless you really need this individual, be prepared to walk away. Are they really pitting different employers against one another or are they trying to get you to increase the offer? There are better negotiating tactics than another (possibly phantom) job offer.

Real World Story

For my first hiring job, I interviewed 22 people for two positions. It was a small working environment with very cramped quarters. When I took over the manager's job, two thirds of the staff had quit the week before.

I did not bring the third person (who was already there) into the hiring process at all, and just informed her once the decision for the other two was made.

The three did not get along immediately and it

required an internal transfer to mollify the situation.

An internal investigation revealed that I had hired two people (neither were American citizens) whose countries are at war with each other (on a different continent).

Talk about circumstances beyond my control.

- *Bank Manager, 25*

I once interviewed for a job and weeks passed without hearing anything. I eventually contacted the company and discovered the hiring manager had been fired *the day after* I had been there.

- *Developer, 31*

Tip 36: Close It Down

Key Points

- You're driving—you started this conversation, it is your job to end it.

- Make sure before you close that you have accomplished some of your key goals.

- Make sure the candidate has had time to ask *you* questions.

- In general, it is not a good idea to mention specific "Next Steps."

- A common way to end interviews— especially initial ones that have gone well— is to give a brief tour of the physical workplace.

Details

You're driving—you started this conversation, it is your job to end it.

- Not only should you decide when the interview starts, you should decide how long it goes and how to end it. The candidate, your fellow interviewers, the next candidate—all these people are waiting on *you*. Not a tremendously large responsibility, but one that a lot of people flub for some reason.

- Be aware that you should structure this whole process well.

Make sure before you close the conversation that you have accomplished some of your key goals.

- In various tips throughout the book, we discuss being prepared. (See <u>Tip 7: Write Down a Job Description</u>, <u>Tip 18: Prepare a List of Questions in Advance,</u> and <u>Tip 27: Take Notes During the Interview</u>.) If you are ready when the interview starts, you should know many of the questions you want answered. You won't get a chance to ask them all, but you should have them ranked (see <u>Tip 18: Prepare a List of Questions in Advance</u>); if your top three questions aren't answered, ask them before you finish with the candidate.

Make sure the candidate has had time to ask *you* questions.

- The more insightful and penetrating the questions the candidate has, the more interested he/she is in your position. Conversely, if they reply that they have no questions, that should be a (small) red flag. It is one thing if the candidate has asked questions during the interview; it is another if they are not curious about anything that was said.

In general, it is not a good idea to mention specific "Next Steps."

- Like any major decision, if you have a little more time to make it, it generally results in a better outcome. Even if the market for talent is boiling hot (see <u>Tip 40: Hiring in Boom and Bust Times</u>), give yourself—and the candidate—at least 24 hours to think about it.

- "You will be hearing from HR." is a standard response. As we discuss early in the book (<u>Tip 2: Talk to HR—or Not</u>), your job is to set the criteria for the correct candidates and conduct the interviews. Other people (HR, generally) should be in charge of the before stuff (weeding the resumes), and the after stuff (following up after the interviews, making the formal job offers, etc.)

A common way to end interviews— especially initial ones that have gone well—is to give a brief tour of the physical workplace.

- Cube farms are cube farms, but it is sometimes a good idea to show them where they will be working. Some environments are wide open; some are tables with long benches; some have many closed offices. The candidate will probably not have a distinct reaction, but they might.

- It is a nice transition into moving the candidate physically out the door.

Remember, you are driving the process, so everyone is waiting on you.

Real World Story

At Facebook headquarters, no one has an enclosed office, *not even the CEO.*

- If you were interviewing for a junior position there, you'd like to know that.

- If you were interviewing for a senior position there, you'd like to know that.

Section C: Hirin'

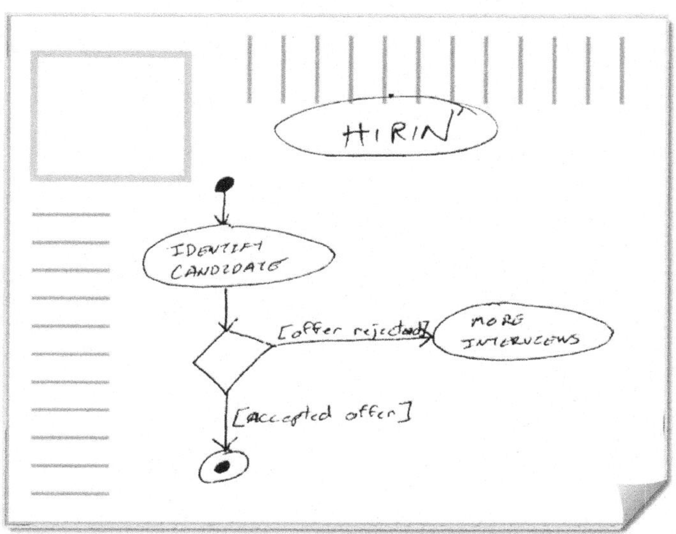

Tip 37: Checking References

Key Points

- This is probably not your job.

- But make sure it is done *before* you make the decision to hire someone.

- Lots of people don't do this, but it is critical that you do it.

- Lots of people cannot say much in response to your call, but make it anyway.

- Here are some questions they can ask when someone else makes these calls for you.

Details

This is probably not your job.

- This is the HR department's job. Many HR departments demand to make these calls. It is not because they love making them (they don't) but because there are legal restrictions on what you can ask and they want to limit your company's liability. Let 'em. Give them some direction and get out of their way.

But make sure it is done *before* you make the decision to hire someone.

- Lots of people don't think this step is important, but it is critical that you do it.

- See <u>Tip 34: Common Hiring Mistakes</u>, for a fuller discussion on why you should not skip this step.

Lots of people cannot say much in response to your call, but make it anyway.

- Many employers will not give out anything besides starting and ending dates. But some will. And you might be surprised at their answers.

Here are some questions they can ask when someone else makes these calls for you:

- "When did Person X work for your company?"

- "Who was their manager?"

- "Did they manage anyone?"

- "Did you work with that person yourself?"

- "Was the company happy or sad to see this person leave?"

Real World Story

I had a job out of college calling references for a company that did reference-checking. I would estimate—I never kept exact numbers—that well over 50% of the people I contacted gave *disapproving* comments about the person I called about. It was seldom super-negative, but it was often things like "Well, if it were up to me, I would not bring this person back on my team" or "I have a hard time saying anything nice about this person." These were contacts provided by the candidates themselves!

- *Project Manager, 45*

Tip 38: Hire Like Your Gonna Have to Eventually Fire 'Em

Key Points

- Not every candidate works out.

- Keep the idea that you may have to fire this person even as you hire them.

- This idea provides a different perspective on a potential employee.

- Hire so that this person can take away your job.

Details

Not every candidate works out.

- They don't work out because the needs of your company changed, they thought the job entailed X but it actually entailed Y, the company suddenly got bought and the new person became expendable, and so on.

- There are many reasons why a person may be fired, and poor performance is only one of them. They *may* turn out to suck at what they do or they may be great performers but they may need to be let go for other reasons.

Keep the idea in mind that you may have to fire this person even as you hire them.

- It sounds strange to say this, but keep in mind the idea that you may have to fire this person even as you hire them. Think about candidates in that context during the interview; it can be of great help to you (and them).

- It would be great if you made new friends every day, but you need to hire for the position, not to find your next BFF.

This idea provides a different perspective on a potential employee.

- You start to think of them as potential liabilities or potential superstars—before you even bring them on to your team!

Hire so that this person so they can take away your job.

- If you say to yourself, "Can this person become so indispensible to my team that I will never be able to fire them? My boss might fire/promote me instead!" that is an excellent candidate you have there.

- If you say to yourself, "I could get rid of this person at the drop of a hat," then maybe you should re-think your decision to even interview this person.

Real World Story

While working for a start-up, we went through a very lean period. Not just the typical hockey stick graph of Q4 revenue with a dry spell the rest of the year, but almost a two-year period with no new sales. Existing customers covered only about 70% of the operating costs, as we had planned on a period of large growth, but changes in the economy suddenly dried up all new customers who were waiting for conditions to change before investing further.

The dreaded term "layoff" was being used in management meetings, and it was clear we would have to cut some team members to keep the company viable in the short-term.

It was an extremely hard task to rank every member of the development staff and figure out just who the company could live without. The decision had been made to cut once, and cut deep. That meant that about 40% of the IT and software development staff would disappear in one day.

Having never faced the thought of letting someone go for any reason but poor performance, it was gut-wrenching to rank each individual. These were my buddies; we had worked hard and played hard together for nearly four years. Heck, I'd even bailed a couple of them out of jail for being drunk and disorderly on a weekend. To say we were all tight was an understatement.

When the layoff day came, we did it quickly and as

professionally as possible. We continued to let them use the office resources (email, copiers, an office, and the phones) for as long as they needed to land another job. We contacted recruiters, who were in the office that day, to interview the folks who were laid off and start the process of finding a new job.

In the end, things worked out. Heck, most landed jobs paying them more than they were making with us!

Still, it was difficult, as the thought of letting someone go had never crossed my mind until that point. Now I'm prepared for the day I have to "free up their future" or tell them it is "time to seek their life's work" as soon as I hire someone. It may seem like a grim perspective, but it is necessary.

- *IT Director, 38*

Tip 39: Don't be Afraid to make 'Em Dance

Key Points

- Making a candidate dance, even just a little bit, is not a bad idea.

- Most jobs have some pressure points.

- Determine how a candidate responds to adversity in the interview.

- Ask how they faced difficult situations in their past.

- This is about them, not about you.

Details

Making a candidate dance, even just a little bit, is not a bad idea.

- While it sounds a bit cruel, making a candidate dance, even just a little bit, is not a bad idea.

- We mean something very specific by 'making them dance.' Obviously, you do not want to see them literally boogie, but there are all kinds of behavioral constraints that you must operate under while interviewing. See Tip 22: What Not to Ask for details about those but read *this* tip for suggestions on how to see how candidates react to various pressure scenarios.

Most jobs have some pressure points.

- Think about it. Unless you are interviewing for a giant retail store greeter, your candidate is going to face some constraints when they take the job. They may face tight deadlines or unclear project requirements or budgetary restraints, but not everything is going to go smoothly.

- You already know some of the problems the candidate may face. You may know that the project you are hiring him or her for is a month late in starting but the finish date has not changed, for example.

- But some challenges are going to appear that neither you nor he or she could have anticipated. (The client company went out of business or the new laptop you ordered for him or her won't be ready by their start date—there are millions of things that could go wrong.)

Determine how a candidate responds to adversity in the interview.

- If you can, determine how a candidate responds to adversity in the interview. One way to do that is to ask some 'what if' questions such as, "How would you handle things if your laptop isn't ready for your start date—and I need you to turn around a project in a week?"

Ask how they faced difficult situations in their past.

- Another technique is to ask how they faced difficult situations in their past. Have them give concrete examples. "We had problems meeting payroll, so I saved the day!" does not count. If a candidate says something like this, they are playing you for a chump. Move on to the next candidate immediately.

- You are looking for something like, "The team had spent a week on this coding problem and no one could figure out how to solve it. One night, while doodling on a napkin, I realized the solution was right in front of our face. I worked all weekend and delivered a new version Monday morning."

This is about them, not about you.

- "Make 'em dance" does *not* mean act like the idiot boss you hated so much in your previous job.

- Keep it in check. You want to see how your potential hire behaves under some pressure, but you want to look yourself in the mirror tomorrow, too. If there are things in your past interviews you did not like, don't repeat them!

Real World Story

Since my group has to present new technologies to the rest of the organization on a regular basis, part of my interview is to present the candidate with a loosely worded problem based upon the type of solutions we have to provide. After presenting the problem, and telling them that they will present their solution when I return, I leave the candidate alone with a white board and give them 15 minutes to come up with a solution.

After 15 minutes, I return. But now I have the others who have interviewed the candidate and two other random developers now playing the role of "project stakeholders" (and introduced as such). Now the candidate not only has to present a decent technical solution, but they are also "on stage" to present to two additional strangers.

There have been some epic candidate meltdowns, as well as some surprisingly great presentations! It's a situation that is common at our company and shows technical ability as well as the capacity to present to an audience all at the same time. All of these are crucial skills to not only develop a solution, but also sell the approach to groups across the organization.

- *Applications Architect Team Lead, 45*

I was in an interview where I was intentionally giving the candidate a hard time. Even though the city where we had both attended different graduate schools was hundreds of miles and many years distant from our current situation, I repeatedly let him know that I thought little of *his* alma mater.

After a while of making him squirm (during which

he appeared to grow more determined to get an offer from me), I suddenly leaned forward and asked him:

- "So, why should I hire you?"

He looked to his left, then his right (we were in the room by ourselves, BTW) and he said:

- "Because I am f***ing tenacious, that's why."

I was surprised—and pleased. I offered him the job on the spot.

- *Technical Product Manager, 45*

Tip 40: Hiring in Boom and Bust Times

As you learn to be a good hiring manager, you'll discover that based on the state of the economy, you'll either have too many candidates or too few. You'll have too many resumes or too few. While different conditions require different skills, great hiring is great hiring. But this Tip will give you some tools for dealing with particular problems caused by economic times.

Key Points

- Boom times: you are so desperate for talent you want to call the local high school.

- Bust times: you get more resumes in your inbox than your Outlook can handle.

- When you are in one type of economic times, you cannot believe there was any other type. But both will occur in your tenure as a hiring manager.

Details

Boom times: you are so desperate for talent you want to call the local high school.

- Don't panic. While you may need a DBA desperately right now, a DBA may be the last thing you need six months from now. It is hard to do, but when you are interviewing, try to think long term.

- Remember that full-time hires are long-term commitments for your company. Most organizations these days have fail-safe processes built in to prevent panic-hires, but you are better off not needing them.

- Read <u>Tip 4: Internal Hires</u> about how to handle the issue of long-term viability of a candidate. Consultants are one option, but there are others.

Bust times: you get more resumes in your inbox than your Outlook can handle.

- Don't panic. You may need a DBA desperately right now, but a DBA may be the last thing you need six months from now. It is hard to do, but when you are interviewing, try to think long term.

- Don't be overwhelmed by the number of resumes or 'perfectly suitable' candidates. In <u>Tip 3: How to Get Help with Your Hiring</u>, we discuss how to get help narrowing the number down.

- Be very prepared. In <u>Tip 7: Write Down a Job Description</u>, we discuss how to write a job description before you start the interviewing process. The cleaner and more defined you make the description, the more suitable (and fewer) the candidates will be that the (internal and/or external) recruiters send you.

- You may or may not want to hire a candidate with more qualifications than you specify. (In <u>Tip 13: Should You Hire an Overqualified Candidate?</u> we discuss this issue in detail.) Sometimes it is a great idea; sometimes it is a terrible idea. Think about this issue *before* you start interviewing.

When you are in one type of economic times, you cannot believe there was any other type. But both will occur in your tenure as a hiring manager.

- It is a cliché that you can't remember when things were so bad. Many psychologists argue that forgetting is a survival mechanism. If we remembered everything, we might not be able to move forward.

Real World Story

Prior to the dot-bomb crash, we had so many applicants (people who looked great on paper and said all the right things) it was amazing. It seemed like things were snowballing out of control in the sense that something new was being introduced every day. Trying to keep the current business afloat and deliver something for a new delivery through a browser was overwhelming. The pace was lightning fast and we needed to get people in the door *right now*.

I helped fill the positions, but not knowing the details of everything meant I was easily fooled.

I can remember one guy who was just nailing it, answering every question with what I thought was spot-on details. I was impressed, and so were the other developers who interviewed him.

Things were great until he started to work. Every day, things were "just a few days" away from being done. Things were 90% done on day one, and stayed that way for months. What was this guy doing all day?

Turned out he was day trading.

No, not checking his 401(k), but actively day trading—all day. We were merely a high-speed Internet connection to him.

He might have had some skills, but we never saw them.

- *Software Developer, 37*

Tip 41: Assign Roles to Co-Interviewers

Key Points

- Everyone involved in the interview should know their role.

- Have someone "assigned" to test their social skills.

Details

Everyone involved in the interview should know their role.

- Don't do the 'good cop/bad cop' thing, but don't wing it, either.

- Give each member of the interview team a list of questions. Ideally, compile the list together.

Have someone assigned to test their social skills.

- Assign one person for the "lunch detail." Their role is to take the candidate out to eat and see how they act in a quasi-social situation. Whether you are going to be eating lunch on a regular basis or not with this person, it is a good idea to see how they behave in a social environment. How do they act toward the wait staff? How do they respond to being asked questions in a public place? You are not looking to see if they know which fork to use, but you are looking for their ability to interact well with others.

Real World Story

Normally I get assigned "lunch duty."

My job was to take the candidate out to lunch and, quote, "see if they were weird." Now, just to be clear, no one expected much weirdness to show up during a straightforward meal, but we were occasionally surprised. We all had stories about candidates who were fine during the office interview but froze up in casual restaurants.

My favorite was the guy who was rude to the waitresses—while we were watching! It didn't take a lot of detective work to figure out how that guy was never going to fit into our team.

- *Civil Engineer, 30*

Tip 42: How Can I Get Better at This?

Key Points

- Interviewing is a learned skill.

- Notice other interviewers as they work.

- Acknowledge that interviewing and hiring are things you have to do, so you might as well get better at it.

- Becoming better at hiring could cut down the "Bozo Quotient" in your office.

- Be careful you're not hiring just clones of yourself.

Details

Interviewing is a learned skill.

- It is not something you are born with. And like any other learned skill, you have to work at it to improve. The fact that you bought this book is a positive first step :-)

- Practice, practice, and more practice. The only way to practice is to do it and do it over and over again. It may feel a little silly, but role-playing with another manager or taking a class on hiring really does help.

Watch what works for other interviewers.

- We have discussed throughout this book the need to have multiple people interview a candidate. While in an interview, you may not consciously notice how other people are asking questions, listening, etc. Make a point of noticing what they are doing. Steal their good techniques—they probably stole them from someone else.

Acknowledge that interviewing and hiring are things you *have* to do...

- ...so you might as well get better at it.

- Get past how busy, important, and famous you are and admit that you need to hire people as part of your job. *You* must hire. (See the intro section: <u>Why You Have to Do This</u>.) So if you *have* to do it, why not do it well? Becoming better at it will make you happier and more effective.

Becoming better at hiring will cut down the "Bozo Quotient" in your office.

- If you are one of the people responsible for bringing people onto your team, you get to vote on whether a candidate is hired. You complain about the "Bozo Quotient" all the time, so now here is your chance to do something about it.

Real World Story

When I was first given a leadership role in a group of software developers, I could hang because scheduling a group was an incremental step up from scheduling myself.

The same was true for estimates, planning a project, and most of the other parts of the job. As long as the staff was constant, I was rocking and rolling, nailing delivery dates and everyone was happy.

Then the company grew. I had to hire more developers. With typical bravado, I thought, "Sure, no problem, I've been interviewed and now I'm just on the other side of the desk. How hard can it be?"

"Real hard" was the answer. I didn't have a clue.

After I had bumbled along for a few interviews and hadn't found anyone, my boss (and company owner) called me into his office and handed me a script. It was his script, filled with coffee stains, tattered edges, and his handwritten notes in the margins.

That document outlined his interview process, the same one I had been interviewed with nearly three years before when I interviewed for my original job at his company—my first job out of college.

I still have that script, pressed between the pages of *The Art of Programming*. I feel his interview script belongs on that same level. I have referred to that piece of paper many times over the years.

I think I needed to be in that almost defeated state
of mind to listen and somehow my boss knew that
I was ready to listen. It wasn't the first time he
kicked my ass (and it wouldn't be the last time,
either).

Looking back, he taught me more theory and
application of theory in four years than all that time
in college ever did. I listened, asked questions,
learned, and practiced what I was taught—over
and over again.

- *Development Team Lead, 32*

Complete List of Key Points

Introduction to Hiring Geeks	**7**
• Who is this book for?	7
• Who should buy this book?	8
• How is this book laid out?	8
• How is each Tip laid out?	9
Why You Have to Do This	**11**
• Why you need to hire.	11
• Why you have to be involved in hiring.	12
• Who do you want to work next to/with?	13
• Being involved in hiring affects Big Picture stuff for you.	13
• Hire the best resource not only for right this minute, but also for the future.	13
• Your team has strengths and weaknesses.	14
• You may be starting a team from scratch, backfilling a position or hiring for a new position due to growth.	15

Tip 1: Always be Looking for Superior Talent. Always.   21

- **The right person suddenly appears at the "wrong" time.**   22
- **Projects seldom go as planned.**   22
- **Life seldom goes as planned.**   22
- **Hiring is like dating.**   23
- **Specifically keep an eye out for out-of-the-box talent.**   23
- **Always.**   23

Tip 2: Talk to HR—or Not   25

- **Some companies have HR departments, some don't.**   25
- **Some companies have *very capable* HR people, some don't.**   26
- **If you have an active, useful HR department, here's why you should *use* them:**   26
- **If you have an inactive, useless HR department, here's why you should *avoid* them:**   26

Tip 3: How to Get Help with Your Hiring   29

- **How much help you get depends on the stage your company is in.**   29
- **Ask for help—your company has people to do this.**   30
- **Use your existing staff.**   31

Tip 4: Internal Hires   33

- Sometimes the stars you are looking for work for your own company… — 33
- Check them out first without a lot of hassle. — 34
- Some managers have been known to read internal forums and sounding boards inside their companies to see how potential internal employees act. — 34

Tip 5: How to Hire Someone Who Has More Technical Knowledge than You — 37

- Let them explain the technology to you. — 37
- Don't try and fake it. — 38
- Ask them how difficult it was to acquire/learn this technology. — 38
- If learning this technology was easily done… — 38
- If they say learning this technology was difficult to do… — 39

Tip 6: Consultant or Employee? — 43

- Decide if you need a consultant or an employee *before* you interview. — 43
- Real quick definitions. — 44
- The line is blurry between consultant and employee. — 45
- If you're in doubt if the position is an employee or a contractor… — 45
- Here's a real example where a consultant is extremely useful. — 46

Tip 7: Write Down a Job Description — 49

- Even if you are an experienced manager that has hired hundreds of people… — 49

- There are many reasons a formal job description is useful. Among them are: 50
- Often HR can either start the process or even do this for you. 50
- You've seen plenty of job descriptions yourself. 51
- Make sure you address the following issues: 51

Tip 8: Using Social Networking 55

- Look on Craigslist! 55
- Look on Facebook... duh. 56
- Look on LinkedIn. 57
- Check MeetUp. 57
- Host hacker face-offs. 58
- Google the job/person/industry 58

Tip 9: Network Your A** Off 61

- While talking to the candidate, keep in mind that he/she probably used their networks to find this interview. 61
- You should use your own network to find the right candidate. 62
- Previous co-workers are a great source of job information. 62
- Other places to look include... 63

Tip 10: The Good, Bad and Ugly about Using Recruiters 65

- Internal recruiters are people who... 65
- External recruiters are people who... 66
- Some companies *require* that you use certain 'recommended' recruiters, or they have 'internal' recruiters. 66

- Recruiters vary radically in skill. (Duh.)   66
- Specifically, most recruiters do not have much technical ability.   67
- External recruiters are generally paid by commission.   67
- You can certainly use multiple recruiters.   68

Tip 11: How to Read a Resume   71

- Check the spelling.   71
- Check out their work history.   72
- Look at the data.   72
- What to do about gaps.   73
- Do the factual claims seem valid?   73

Tip 12: Narrowing Down the List (Initial Step)   77

- No one can do this easily. Luckily, it is probably not your job to do it anyway.   77
- And they are not doing it manually (or they shouldn't be, anyway).   78
- If you don't have an HR department, you need to find help.   78
- Toss all resumes that: 78

Tip 13: Should You Hire an Overqualified Candidate?   83

- These candidates require special attention from their manager.   84
- For one thing, an over-qualified candidate may just be 'parking it for a little while.'   84
- Another issue is that some people get bored easily.   84
- Experienced managers can often head this problem off.   85

- But be careful if you are not up for this level of challenge.   85

Section B: Interviewin'   *87*

Tip 14: Conduct the Best Type of Interview   89

- When the *candidate* determines as honestly as they can...   90
- When the *company* determines as honestly as they can...   90
- ...how well they fit together.   90
- It is fairly common to ask this question directly: 91
- Just as common is for them to ask you this question: 91
- Remember, the perfect interview is when...   92
- See Tip 33: When and How to *Stop* an Interview on how to bring an interview to an end before it is scheduled to finish.   93
- See Tip 36: Close It Down on how to finish an interview well.   93

Tip 15: Useful Interview Guidelines   95

- The candidate may be nervous—some people cannot relax in an interview setting and that nervousness may not reflect their skill level.   95
- Some people are shy—very, very shy. A lot of geeks are shy.   96
- Don't talk the whole time! See Tip 34: Common Hiring Mistakes for more detail on this topic.   96
- Try to avoid simple questions with a "yes" or "no" answer.   97

- Always give the candidate some time to ask their own questions.   97
- Notice how well they present themselves.   98

Tip 16: Let Management Know What You Need   101

- Make the justification as quantitative as you can.   101
- If possible, quantify the (potential) new hire's role.   102

Tip 17: How to Greet Interviewees   105

- Be respectful of the candidate.   105
- Greet them promptly.   106
- Get over the initial jitters.   106

Tip 18: Prepare a List of Questions in Advance   109

- Compile a list of questions you need to know about every candidate *before* you go into the interview.   110
- Sort that list.   110
- Do they have soft skills?   110
- Can you imagine working *with* this person or even *for* this person?   110
- No interviewee in the history of mankind was perfect.   111
- Give the list of questions to the other interviewers.   111

Tip 19: Basic Questions to Cover   113

- How many years of experience using the technology in question do they have?   113
- Do they have a college degree?   114
- What kind of training/certification do they have?   114

- What specific hardware and software technologies are they familiar with?   114
- How many years of work experience do they have?   115
- Have two very specific questions you got from looking at their resume.   115
- Choose a few of these general questions.   115

Tip 20: Ask Open-Ended Questions   119

- Problem solving, and software development in particular, isn't just about syntax.   120
- There are a lot of charlatans who could snow you in a brief interview.   120
- The skills and experience they have may not be exactly what you think you're looking for.   121
- Ask probing questions to uncover unexpected information.   122
- You have limited time to make the hiring decision.   122
- Listen for "I" statements.   123

Tip 21: Nontechnical Questions   125

- Here are some sample nontechnical topics you can raise and questions you can ask: 125

Tip 22: What *Not* to Ask   129

- Some very specific questions are illegal to ask a candidate in an interview.   129
- Here is a list of federally mandated topics to avoid: 129
- The liability for violating these laws is significant. Don't play games with this.   130

Tip 23: Who Else Should Interview a Candidate?   133

- **Who else can help me interview candidates?**   134
- **Should you bring in the team at the very introductory stage?**   134
- **Should you have a semi-formal 'good cop/bad cop' routine?**   135
- **What if some people do not want to do this?**   135
- **How many people should a candidate interview with?**   136

Tip 24: Value of Certification   137

- **Some jobs absolutely require a certification.**   137
- **Check out how valuable a particular certification is.**   138
- **It lets you know the candidate knows the basics but it does not let you know if they can think on their own.**   139
- **Can they solve problems on their own?**   139
- **Some certificates require persistence, which in and of itself is a good thing.**   140

Tip 25: Value of Commitment   143

- **Some people just coast through life.**   143
- **One way to test their commitment level is to evaluate the length of time the candidate has spent at a company.**   144
- **See if they stand for something away from the keyboard.**   144
- **Some people read the 'personal' section of resumes first.**   145

Tip 26: Value of Education   147

- Some famous and rich guys in IT did not graduate from college. 147
- Not all college degrees and college majors are created the same. 148
- Use education as a weeding factor. 148
- "How valuable—how *directly* valuable—is education to the job at hand?" is perhaps the wrong question. 149
- Should you care about famous schools? 149
- Do soft skills matter in an IT job? 150
- Are you asking for an advanced degree? 151

Tip 27: Take Notes *During* the Interview 153

- Sometimes you don't have time to prepare a list of questions before you interview. 154
- Do a little work in advance or you might miss some very important facts. 154
- Some people are brilliant interviewers. 155
- After you interview five candidates, they start to blur. 155
- Be careful how you take notes. 155
- Regardless, you should *always* scribble a few notes after *every* interview. 155

Tip 28: Offering the Correct Amount for an IT Position 157

- Your hiring budget gives you a place to start. 157
- Recruiters are a great source of information. 158
- Your current employees can be a valuable supply of contacts. 159

- The candidates themselves, amazingly, can often be good resources.   **159**

Tip 29: Other Ideas Besides More Money   **161**

- Sometimes geeks want other things besides money.   **162**
- Time off is important, too.   **163**
- Non-standard benefits can be very valuable to some people.   **163**
- Variable compensation is another valuable idea some employees love.   **164**

Tip 30: Have a "D-IQ" (Developer IQ)   **167**

- You may have to cover a lot of ground in a short amount of time.   **167**
- A little knowledge about a lot of things is good.   **168**
- Keep it quick and have fun.   **169**
- Ask how they feel about a particular technology.   **169**
- Questions for someone who needed at least a passing familiarity with RDBMS and SQL include: **169**

Tip 31: Things to Watch Out For   **173**

- There are many people who over-promise and under-deliver.   **173**
- Are the facts on their resume correct? (See Tip 11: How to Read a Resume.)   **174**
- Have they ever completed anything in their lives?   **174**
- A classic hiring landmine statement is: "I never knew I had to…"   **175**
- Personal hygiene issues are tricky but they can be critical, too.   **176**

- Advance degree holders want more $$ for their extra coursework. 176

Tip 32: Watch Out for the New Guy Who Can't Code 179

- You need to hire smart people who get things done. 179
- Don't hire inept people. 180
- New hires can frustrate you. 180

Tip 33: When and How to *Stop* an Interview 183

- Your time is valuable. 183
- Like meetings, job interviews can go *less* than their allotted time. 183
- Sometimes, go the allotted length. 184
- Sometimes, cut it off quickly. 184
- Sometimes, let it go over. 184
- What is the right length of time for an interview? The answer (obviously) is "It depends." 185

Tip 34: Common Hiring Mistakes 187

- Don't define the position poorly. 187
- Don't hire for political reasons instead of valid team and required skill ones. 188
- Don't talk the whole time. 188
- Don't neglect the background checking stuff. 189
- Be careful you're not just hiring clones of yourself. 190

Tip 35: It Might Not Go Well Anyway 191

- Things seldom go according plan. 191
- *Your* circumstances could change. 191
- *Their* circumstances could change. 192

Tip 36: Close It Down   195

- You're driving—you started this conversation, it is your job to end it.   195
- Make sure before you close the conversation that you have accomplished some of your key goals.   196
- Make sure the candidate has had time to ask *you* questions.   196
- In general, it is not a good idea to mention specific "Next Steps."   197
- A common way to end interviews— especially initial ones that have gone well—is to give a brief tour of the physical workplace.   197

Section C: Hirin'   199

Tip 37: Checking References   201

- This is probably not your job.   201
- But make sure it is done *before* you make the decision to hire someone.   202
- Lots of people cannot say much in response to your call, but make it anyway.   202
- Here are some questions they can ask when someone else makes these calls for you: 202

Tip 38: Hire Like Your Gonna Have to Eventually Fire 'Em   205

- Not every candidate works out.   205
- Keep the idea in mind that you may have to fire this person even as you hire them. 206
- This idea provides a different perspective on a potential employee.   206

- Hire so that this person so they can take away your job.   206

Tip 39: Don't be Afraid to make 'Em Dance   209

- Making a candidate dance, even just a little bit, is not a bad idea.   209
- Most jobs have some pressure points.   210
- Determine how a candidate responds to adversity in the interview.   210
- Ask how they faced difficult situations in their past.   211
- This is about them, not about you.   211

Tip 40: Hiring in Boom and Bust Times   215

- Boom times: you are so desperate for talent you want to call the local high school.   215
- Bust times: you get more resumes in your inbox than your Outlook can handle.   216
- When you are in one type of economic times, you cannot believe there was any other type. But both will occur in your tenure as a hiring manager.   217

Tip 41: Assign Roles to Co-Interviewers   219

- Everyone involved in the interview should know their role.   219
- Have someone assigned to test their social skills.   219

Tip 42: How Can I Get Better at This?   221

- Interviewing is a learned skill.   221
- Watch what works for other interviewers.   222
- Acknowledge that interviewing and hiring are things you *have* to do…   222

- **Becoming better at hiring will cut down the "Bozo Quotient" in your office.**   **222**

Complete List of Key Points   *225*

Made in the USA
Monee, IL
07 July 2026